# Retirement Mess To Retirement Success

## Lessons Learned from Retirees And How to Avoid Their Regrets

ILYNMW Publishing
Atlanta Georgia

paulbeersdorf@gmail.com

Published by: ILYNMW Publishing

V21.0



During the writing of the book, the author used Google Gemini, Microsoft CoPilot, ChatGPT and Grammarly to help with chapter content, ideation, style, grammar and structure.

Cover Design: Paul Beersdorf

**ISBN: 978-1-971344-05-8**

## Disclaimer and Terms of Use

The content of this book is for educational, informational, and entertainment purposes only. The insights, anecdotes, and observations contained herein are compiled from the subjective thoughts, opinions, experiences, and regrets of retired individuals. They do not constitute universal facts, nor do they represent individual, personalized professional counsel.

No Professional Advice: The author and publisher are not engaged in rendering legal, financial, investment, tax, psychological, or medical advice. Because every individual's financial situation, tax bracket, physical health, and personal circumstances are completely unique, the information in this book should not be used as a substitute for consultation with competent, licensed professionals.

Prior to making any major financial transitions, altering investment portfolios, implementing tax strategies, making real estate decisions, or modifying health and fitness routines, readers are strongly urged to consult with a Certified Financial Planner (CFP), Certified Public Accountant (CPA), qualified attorney, or licensed physician.

**Limitation of Liability:** While every effort has been made to ensure the accuracy of the information compiled at the time of publication, the author and publisher assume no responsibility or liability for any errors, omissions, or contrary interpretations of the subject matter. The reader assumes full responsibility for the use of these materials and any outcomes resulting from actions taken based on the content of this book.

# Books by Paul Beersdorf

Flowers on Tuesday
52 Things I Wish My Father Had Told Me about Marriage and Family
The 100 Most Important Words
Encouraging Your Wife
Encouraging Your Husband
Advice for Today, Tomorrow and Forever
Even Moses Needed Encouragement
Storm Management
Living Intentionally
Luck, Chance or Prayer
Choosing to Finish Well
Destination - Dad 2.0
Characteristics of a Leader
Unleadership
Character of God - Devotional
Parents, Prodigals and Prayer - Devotional
The Command Habit - Devotional
A Song in Your Step - Devotional

# Table of Contents

# Dedication

This book is dedicated to my beautiful Bride Debbie!

I love my Beautiful Bride and how much she encourages me to write and share my thoughts and ideas. She is the love of my life and my best friend. Nothing I do would be worthwhile without her by my side.

I love you no matter what!
You are the love of my life!
You are my best friend ever seen!
All of me loves all of you!
You are the only one for me!
You are the desire of my heart!
You captivate my heart!
You complete me and make me a better man!
If I had to choose all over again, I would choose you!
Thanks for saying yes!
I choose you!
143

# Introduction

I primarily wrote this book for myself. It is a true labor of love—the culmination of seven years of intense research, interviews, and deep reflection.

Although I am now retired, I first started deeply analyzing my next steps when I turned fifty-five. Because I didn't have a personal blueprint or a retired role model to turn to for guidance, I decided to build my own.

I interviewed friends and family who had already successfully crossed the finish line, surveyed other retirees, watched hundreds of educational videos, and devoured countless articles, books, financial blogs, and academic research papers.

The good news is that the world is flooded with retirement data. The bad news? I couldn't find a single, consolidated master checklist of what to do and—just as importantly—what *not* to do. Much of the mainstream advice was contradictory, generic, and failed to account for unique individual circumstances.

As I write these words, I am sitting in a condo in Hawaii, looking out the window at the Pacific surf crashing onto the beach. Some might view this as a boast or a "flex." But what I truly want you to see is that I am simply practicing exactly what I preach in this book.

Before conducting this research, I had three major blind spots that these chapters helped me cure:

1. **Enjoying the "Go-Go" Years:** One critical piece of advice I had never considered was the urgency of traveling and taking on physically demanding adventures while I am still young and mobile. That insight is exactly why my wife and I came to Hawaii to celebrate our 36th wedding anniversary—to hike, explore, and island-hop across the Big Island while we are in peak health.

2. **Breaking the Saving Compulsion:** My natural instinct has always been to *save, save, save*. After forty-five years of accumulating wealth, flipping the switch to start spending your hard-earned portfolio is terrifying. But the collective wisdom of real retirees was clear: spend more during your active early retirement years to build priceless memories, rather than hoarding capital until the very end.

3. **Establishing a Retirement Purpose:** True retirement requires a renewed sense of purpose. Writing has become a vital creative outlet and a defining pillar of my daily purpose. I hope these pages illuminate your path, but at a bare minimum, the act of writing them has completely transformed mine.

Undertaking this massive research project exposed the deep blind spots in my initial strategy and forced me to re-evaluate plans I foolishly assumed would work. My hope is that this guide serves as a practical, educational companion as you design your own future.

Just remember: one size never fits all. What works beautifully for my life might not align with yours. Do your own homework, assemble a trusted team of professionals, and become a true student of retirement.

Let me be completely clear before you dive any deeper into this book.

I am not a lawyer. I am not an accountant or a CPA. I am not a Certified Financial Planner (CFP) or an insurance agent. I am not a physician, nurse, or healthcare professional. I am not a real estate agent, a relationship expert, or a counselor. I am not trying to sell you anything!

Simply put: I am just a man who wanted to uncover the hidden pitfalls of retirement before stepping into them myself. More importantly, I wanted genuine advice from those who had already been there, done that, and earned the t-shirt. The wisdom shared in these pages is for general knowledge and educational purposes only.

Everyone's retirement is fundamentally unique. The chapters ahead contain the hindsight, hard-learned lessons, and daily success stories of seniors who have already crossed the finish line of full-time work—sharing what worked for them and what they wish they had done differently.

However, please remember that this is a book of ***perspectives,*** not **prescriptions.**

Your financial picture, your health, your family dynamics, and your personal goals belong uniquely to you. What was a masterstroke for one retiree might be an absolute mess for another, depending on your tax brackets, timelines, and risk tolerance. Use this wisdom as a guide to spark ideas, ask better questions, and spot your own potential blind spots—but always run your final plans by your own trusted team of financial, legal, and medical professionals before you officially pull the trigger.

# Milestones

I wanted to start this book with a quick discussion on age milestones. What I mean by that is all the special ages and time periods you have to consider before and during retirement. As with the rest of this book, I am not going to go into great detail, but instead give you some general understanding and outlines. This may seem boring and mundane, but it is critically important for you to understand each of these milestones and the impact they can have on your retirement.

**Here is a brief outline and then more details about each age milestone:**

**20's, 30's & 40's – Saving and building retirement nest egg**
**Age 50 – "Catch-up" funding for retirement savings**
**Age 55 – "Catch-up" funding for HSA account**
**Age 55 – Tap in to work 401k without penalty (special rules apply)**
**Age 59 ½ - tap into IRA without 10% penalty**
**Age 62 – Take social security early (but with penalty)**
**Age 63 – Look back age for Medicare income requirement**
**Age 65 – Sign up for Medicare**
**Age 67 – Full retirement age for social security (no penalty)**
**Age 70 – Final age to take social security (24% bonus for waiting)**
**Age 70 ½ - age you can use QCD (qualified charitable distribution)**
**70 ½ 72, 73, 75 – age when RMD's become due (based on your birthdate)**

## 20's, 30's & 40's

These are the ages when you should be putting away money in your IRA, 401K, Roth accounts and or other retirement vehicles. You should be taking full advantage of your employers matching programs. In my case I consistently saved 15% of my income from every paycheck.

You might want to consider developing a relationship with a fee-only certified financial planner (CFP) and investing some money in their advice.

# AGE 50

At age 50 you should start looking at your retirement portfolio and consider how much risk you are willing to take. You now have fewer years until retirement and cannot afford to take big losses in your retirement portfolio.

This is also the age when you can start to do "catch up" saving for retirement:

• 401(k) catch-ups – You can contribute above the standard limit; in 2026 the catch-up amount is $8,000.
• 403(b) catch-ups – Same age-50 catch-up applies.
• 457(b) catch-ups – Standard age-50 catch-up applies.
• IRA catch-ups – Traditional & Roth IRAs allow an extra $1,100 in 2026.
• SIMPLE IRA catch-ups – Extra $4,000 in 2026.

(Remember, all of these are subject to change. These are based on 2026 laws)

# AGE 55

Under current laws in the USA, this is the first age when you can consider taking early retirement and tapping into to retirement savings without a penalty (however, there are specific rules and regulations)

Tapping into retirement accounts before the standard age of 59½ usually triggers a 10% early withdrawal penalty. However, if you are looking to access funds between the ages of 55 and 59½, the IRS provides specific pathways to bypass that penalty.

Ordinary income taxes will still apply to any pre-tax distributions—only the 10% early withdrawal penalty is waived.

What follows are more specific insights into the "Rule of 55"

# 1. The "Rule of 55" (Workplace Plans Only)

The most common way to access funds at this stage is the **Rule of 55**. This provision allows you to withdraw money penalty-free from an employer-sponsored retirement plan if you leave your job early.

- **The Timing:** You must separate from service (whether you retire, quit, are laid off, or are fired) **during or after the calendar year you turn 55**.
- **The Plan Limitation:** This rule applies **only** to the 401(k) or 403(b) plan associated with the employer you just left. It cannot be used to access traditional IRAs, Roth IRAs, or old 401(k) plans left behind at previous employers (unless you rolled those old accounts into your current workplace plan before separating).
- **Plan Discretion:** Employers are not required by law to offer flexible withdrawals under this rule. Some company plans allow you to take partial distributions as needed, while others might force a rigid "all-or-nothing" lump-sum payout, which can unintentionally push you into a higher tax bracket.

# 2. Rule 72(t) / SEPP (IRAs & Workplace Plans)

If your money is already tied up in a traditional or Roth IRA, the Rule of 55 will not apply. Instead, you can use **Substantially Equal Periodic Payments (SEPP)** under Internal Revenue Code Section 72(t).

- **The Mechanism:** You commit to pulling a fixed amount of money out of your account annually, calculated using one of three IRS-approved life expectancy tables.
- **The Timeline:** Once you start, you must stick to this exact schedule for **five years or until you reach age 59½, whichever is longer**.
- **The Risk:** SEPP schedules are incredibly rigid. If you change the withdrawal amount, skip a year, or cancel the plan early, the IRS

retroactively applies the 10% penalty to *all* previous withdrawals, plus interest.

## Comparing Your Early Access Options

| **Feature** | **The Rule of 55** | **Rule 72(t) (SEPP)** |
|---|---|---|
| **Account Type** | Current 401(k) or 403(b) only | IRAs, 401(k)s, and 403(b)s |
| **Employment Status** | Must leave that specific employer at age 55 or later | Can be employed or retired |
| **Withdrawal Flexibility** | High (take varying amounts as needed, if the plan permits) | Low (locked into a strict, calculated annual amount) |
| **Commitment** | None (stop and start as you please) | Minimum 5 years or until age 59½ |

## 3. Alternative Penalty-Free Outlets

**Governmental 457(b) Plans:** If you have a 457(b) plan from a state or local government job, these accounts are entirely exempt from the 10% early withdrawal penalty upon separation from service, regardless of your age.

**Roth IRA Contributions:** You can always withdraw your original *contributions* to a Roth IRA tax-free and penalty-free at any age for any reason. Only the *earnings* (the growth) are subject to taxes and a penalty if withdrawn before age 59½.

Before making a structural change or requesting a distribution, checking the specific summary plan description (SPD) of the workplace account will confirm exactly how that specific administrator processes early departures.

## HSA Catch-up

At age 55 you also get the opportunity to do HSA (Health Savings Account) catch up. Under current law, you can contribute an additional $1,000 each year, on top of your normal contribution.

# AGE 59 ½

This is the first age when you can tap into your retirement savings without taking a 10% penalty

# AGE 62

This is the first age when you can claim social security early. However, you need to understand that you will encounter a PERMANENT reduction in your social security benefit.

For anyone born in 1960 or later, the Full Retirement Age (FRA) is 67. Claiming your Social Security benefits at this exact age guarantees you receive 100% of your primary insurance amount (your baseline benefit).

Filing early results in a permanent monthly reduction, while waiting past age 67 locks in guaranteed annual increases up until age 70.

## The Year-by-Year Breakdown (FRA = 67)

| Claiming Age | % of Your Full Benefit | Total Reduction or Gain | How the Shift is Calculated |
|---|---|---|---|
| **62** | 70.0% | **-30.0%** | Baseline minus maximum early filing penalty |
| **63** | 75.0% | **-25.0%** | Reduced by an extra 5.0% per year for months 37 to 60 early |
| **64** | 80.0% | **-20.0%** | Reduced by 6.67% per year for the first 36 months early |
| **65** | 86.7% | **-13.3%** | Reduced by 6.67% per year for the first 36 months early |
| **66** | 93.3% | **-6.7%** | Reduced by 6.67% per year for the first 36 months early |

| Claiming Age | % of Your Full Benefit | Total Reduction or Gain | How the Shift is Calculated |
|---|---|---|---|
| **67 (FRA)** | **100.0%** | **Baseline (0%)** | **No reduction, no bonus** |
| **68** | 108.0% | **+8.0%** | Earns 8.0% delayed retirement credit per year |
| **69** | 116.0% | **+16.0%** | Earns 8.0% delayed retirement credit per year |
| **70** | 124.0% | **+24.0%** | Maximum delayed credits accumulated |

# How the SSA Calculates the Math

The Social Security Administration (SSA) does not use flat annual rates; they calculate reductions and gains on a **month-by-month** basis to account for the exact month you file:

- **The First 36 Months Early (Ages 64 to 66):** Benefits are reduced by **5/9 of 1%** for each month you claim early. This adds up to a **6.67% reduction per year**.

- **Beyond 36 Months Early (Ages 62 and 63):** Benefits are reduced by an additional **5/12 of 1%** for each month. This adds up to a **5.0% reduction per year**.
- **Delayed Credits (Ages 68 to 70):** For every month you delay past age 67, your benefit increases by **2/3 of 1%**. This adds up to a clean **8.0% increase per year**.

The benefits stop growing once you hit age 70, so there is no financial incentive to wait past your 70th birthday.

# AGE 63

If you plan to enroll in Medicare at age 65, you need to know that the federal government implements a strict **two-year lookback** to determine your premiums. This means your income at age sixty-three dictates your healthcare costs at sixty-five.

Specifically, Medicare looks at your Modified Adjusted Gross Income (MAGI) to determine if you must pay extra for your coverage. If your income crosses certain federal thresholds, Medicare tacks an additional surcharge onto your Part B (medical insurance) and Part D (prescription drug) premiums. This surcharge is known as the **Income-Related Monthly Adjustment Amount (IRMAA)**, and it can easily catch unsuspecting retirees off guard.

## How Medicare Defines MAGI

Medicare's version of MAGI is very straightforward, but it features a major trap for investors who assume tax-exempt income is safe. To find your Medicare MAGI, the government takes your standard **Adjusted Gross Income (AGI)** from your tax return and adds just one primary thing back:

{Medicare MAGI} = {AGI} + {Tax-Exempt Interest Income}

**The Municipal Bond Trap:** While interest from municipal bonds is exempt from federal income taxes (and does not increase your standard AGI), it **is**

added back to calculate your MAGI for Medicare. Generating substantial tax-free interest can accidentally trigger higher Medicare premiums.

### What is Included in Your MAGI?

- Wages, business income, and taxable pensions
- Traditional IRA withdrawals and traditional 401(k)/403(b) distributions
- Capital gains (realized from selling stocks, funds, or property)
- Taxable dividends and regular interest
- The taxable portion of your Social Security benefits
- **Tax-exempt interest** (like municipal bond yields)

### What is Excluded from Your MAGI?

- Qualified Roth IRA or Roth 401(k) distributions
- Qualified Health Savings Account (HSA) distributions used for medical costs
- Life insurance payouts

## The Two-Year Look-back Rule

Medicare doesn't look at your current calendar year income to determine your premiums. Instead, it uses a mandatory **two-year lookback window** because your most recent, fully processed tax return is what the IRS has on file.

- Your **2026** Medicare premiums are entirely based on your **2024** tax return.

- Your **2027** Medicare premiums will be based on your **2025** tax return.

This delay means financial moves made in early retirement (like taking a massive multi-year capital gain or doing large Roth conversions) will hit your healthcare expenses exactly two years down the road.

## The 2026 Initial IRMAA Thresholds

If your MAGI falls at or below the initial thresholds, you pay the standard base premium (which is **$202.90 per month** for Part B). If you go even $1 over these lines, you cross a strict "tax cliff" into higher premium brackets:

- **Individual / Single Filers:** $109,000 or less
- **Married Filing Jointly:** $218,000 or less

***Note: If you experience a sudden drop in income due to a major life-changing event (such as formal retirement, a work reduction, or the loss of income-producing property), you don't have to wait two years for the system to catch up. You can file Form SSA-44 with the Social Security Administration to request an immediate reduction of your premium surcharge.***

# AGE 65

This is the first age for you to sign up for Medicare.

The standard age to become eligible for Medicare is **65**.

While enrolling is a major milestone, the program has strict timeline rules. Unless you qualify to delay coverage because you are still working and covered by a large employer plan, missing your initial enrollment window triggers permanent, lifelong premium penalties.

# The Medicare Enrollment Windows

Your timeline for signing up without penalty depends on three specific windows:

- **Initial Enrollment Period (IEP):** This is a **7-month window** centered around your 65th birthday. It includes the 3 months before you turn 65, the month of your birthday, and the 3 months after.
- **Special Enrollment Period (SEP):** If you or your spouse are still actively working at age 65 and have health coverage through an employer group health plan (typically at a company with 20 or more employees), you can safely delay Medicare. Once that job or coverage ends, you have an **8-month window** to sign up for Part A and Part B, and a **63-day window** to sign up for Part D, penalty-free.
- **General Enrollment Period (GEP):** If you miss your IEP or SEP, you can only sign up between **January 1 and March 31** each year. Your coverage begins the month after you enroll, and late penalties will likely be added to your bills.

# The Penalties for Missing Your Window

Medicare penalties are calculated differently for each "Part" of the program. For Parts B and D, these are not one-time late fees—they are permanent premium surcharges that you pay for life.

## 1. Part A Penalty (Hospital Insurance)

Most Americans get Part A for free because they (or their spouse) paid Medicare taxes for at least 40 work quarters (about 10 years). However, if you do not qualify for premium-free Part A and miss your enrollment window:

- **The Penalty:** Your monthly Part A premium increases by **10%**.

- **The Duration:** You must pay this higher premium for **twice the number of full years** you delayed enrollment. (For example, if you were eligible but didn't sign up for 2 years, you will pay the 10% penalty for 4 years).

## 2. Part B Penalty (Medical Insurance)

Because Part B requires a monthly premium from everyone, the IRS and Medicare strictly penalize delays to keep healthy people from waiting until they get sick to enroll.

- **The Penalty:** A permanent **10% increase** for every full 12-month period you could have had Part B but didn't sign up.
- **The Duration: Lifetime**. The penalty stays on your premium for as long as you have Medicare.
- **2026 Cost Example:** The standard Part B premium is **$202.90 per month**. If you delay enrollment by two full years (24 months), you will face a 20% penalty. This adds an extra $40.58 to your bill every single month, bringing your total monthly premium to $243.48.

## 3. Part D Penalty (Prescription Drug Coverage)

Even if you do not currently take prescription medications, you must enroll in a bare-minimum Part D plan or hold "creditable" drug coverage (coverage deemed as good as Medicare's by your insurer) to avoid a future penalty.

- **The Penalty:** An extra **1% for every full month** you go without Part D or creditable coverage, provided you go 63 days or more without it.
- **The Calculation:** The percentage is multiplied by the "national base beneficiary premium," which changes slightly every year. For 2026, the base premium is **$38.99**.
- **The Duration: Lifetime**.
- **2026 Cost Example:** If you go 14 months without drug coverage after your IEP ends, your penalty will be 14% of $38.99. This adds an extra $5.50 per month (rounded to the nearest dime) onto whatever Part D plan premium you choose, adjusting slightly each year as the national base fluctuates.

# Penalty Summary Table

| Medicare Part | Who is At Risk? | Penalty Amount | How Long It Lasts |
|---|---|---|---|
| **Part A** | Those with fewer than 40 work quarters who must buy Part A | 10% premium surcharge | Twice the number of years you delayed |
| **Part B** | Anyone without a qualifying employer group plan past age 65 | 10% surcharge per full 12-month period delayed | **Permanently for life** |
| **Part D** | Anyone without creditable prescription drug coverage for 63+ days | 1% surcharge per month delayed (based on national base premium) | **Permanently for life** |

**The COBRA Trap:** A common and costly mistake is assuming COBRA or retiree health insurance counts as "active employment coverage." It does not. If you leave your job at age 65 or later and opt for COBRA, the 8-month window to enroll in Part B without a penalty starts the month your active employment ends, *not* when your COBRA runs out.

# AGE 67

This is the full retirement age for everyone born after 1960 - which will be the vast majority of you who are reading this book. This is when you can take your social security without any penalty.

# AGE 70

This is the age when there is no benefit to waiting any longer for social security. If you have waited this long, you now get 24% more social security and that is locked in for life

# AGE 70 ½

This is the age when you can start taking advantage of QCD (Qualified Charitable Donations). In short, this is a rule that allows you to give money directly from your IRA retirement funds without it impacting you income or taxes. It can also help satisfy all or part of your RMD (required minimum distributions)

A **Qualified Charitable Distribution (QCD)** is a tax-advantaged strategy that allows individuals who are **70½ years old or older** to transfer funds directly from their Individual Retirement Account (IRA) to an eligible public charity.

Instead of taking a distribution as taxable income and then donating it, the money moves seamlessly from the IRA custodian to the non-profit. For the 2026 tax year, the IRS allows an individual to donate up to **$111,000** annually through QCDs.

If you are married, both you and your spouse can split this benefit for a total of up to $222,000, provided you both meet the age requirement and have separate IRAs.

# The Pros of a QCD

- **Lowers Your Adjusted Gross Income (AGI):** Because the distribution goes directly to the charity, it never enters your gross income. A lower AGI can keep you in a lower tax bracket and protect you from high-income tax triggers, such as Medicare premium surcharges (IRMAA) or taxes on Social Security benefits.
- **Satisfies Your RMDs:** Once you reach age (70 ½ , 72, 73 or 75) and are hit with Required Minimum Distributions (RMDs), a QCD counts toward fulfilling that mandatory annual withdrawal, allowing you to meet your legal obligation without inflating your income.
- **No Itemization Required:** Normally, to get a tax break for charity, you have to itemize your deductions on Schedule A. With a QCD, you can claim the standard deduction and *still* get the full tax exclusion on your donated retirement assets.
- **Bypasses New 2026 Tax Hurdles:** Under current 2026 tax rules, itemized charitable contributions face a new 0.5% AGI floor (meaning you can only deduct gifts that exceed 0.5% of your income), and high earners see their deduction benefits capped. A QCD completely bypasses these new restrictions because it is treated as excluded income rather than a tax deduction.

# The Cons of a QCD

- **Strict Age Floor:** The IRS is unyielding on the age requirement. You must be at least **70½ years old on the exact day** the distribution is made. Initiating a transfer even a few days before hitting 70½ turns the transaction into a standard, fully taxable withdrawal.

- **No "Double Dipping":** Because the distribution is already excluded from your taxable income, you cannot double-count it by claiming a charitable tax deduction on your tax return.

- **Account Limitations:** QCDs can only be executed from an IRA (Traditional, Rollover, Inherited, or inactive SEP and SIMPLE IRAs). You cannot make a QCD directly from an active workplace plan like a 401(k) or a 403(b).

- **Destination Restrictions:** The funds must go directly to a qualified 501(c)(3) public charity. You cannot use a QCD to fund a Donor-Advised Fund (DAF), a private foundation, or a supporting organization.

- **Zero Personal Benefit:** You cannot receive any goods or services in exchange for the donation. If your QCD covers the cost of a charity gala ticket or a charity auction item, the entire distribution becomes disqualified.

# Comparing QCDs vs. Traditional Cash Donations

| **Feature** | **Qualified Charitable Distribution (QCD)** | **Traditional Cash Donation** |
|---|---|---|
| **Minimum Age** | 70½ | None |
| **How It Reduces Tax** | Excludes the amount from taxable income entirely | Provides an itemized tax deduction |
| **Tax Filing Strategy** | Works perfectly with the Standard Deduction | Requires Itemizing on Schedule A to see any benefit |
| **2026 Tax Rules Impact** | Exempt from the 0.5% AGI floor and high-income caps | Fully subject to the 0.5% AGI floor and deduction caps |
| **Fulfills RMD?** | Yes | No |

# AGES 70 ½, 72 , 73 or 75

These are the ages when you will be need to take your required minimum distribution. The government allowed you to grow your retirement funds tax free for years and now they want their portion of the taxes. This is their way of forcing distributions so they can get their taxes!

A **Required Minimum Distribution (RMD)** is the legally mandated minimum amount of money that you must withdraw each year from your tax-deferred retirement accounts.

Because traditional IRAs, 401(k)s, and 403(b)s grow using pre-tax dollars, the IRS institutes RMDs to ensure it eventually collects income tax on those assets.

Under current tax laws established by the SECURE Act 2.0, lifetime RMD requirements apply to traditional IRAs and pre-tax workplace plans. Roth IRAs are entirely exempt from lifetime RMDs, and starting in recent years, designated Roth accounts within employer 401(k) and 403(b) plans are also exempt from lifetime RMD rules.

**The First-Year Deadline Rule:** Your very first RMD must be taken by **April 1 of the calendar year following** the year you reach your required age. However, waiting until April 1 means you must take *two* distributions in a single tax year (your first-year delayed RMD plus your current-year RMD due by December 31), which can severely spike your taxable income. All subsequent RMDs must be taken by December 31 each year.

## When Must You Begin? RMD Age by Birth Year

The age at which you are legally forced to start taking distributions depends entirely on the year you were born. Congress has steadily pushed this age back over recent legislative sessions:

| Year of Birth | Required RMD Starting Age | Legislation |
|---|---|---|
| **Before July 1, 1949** | 70½ | Original Tax Code |
| **July 1, 1949 - Dec 31, 1950** | 72 | SECURE Act 1.0 (2019) |
| **1951 - 1959** | 73 | SECURE Act 2.0 (2022) |
| **1960 or later** | 75 | SECURE Act 2.0 (2022) |

# IRS Uniform Lifetime Table (Ages 73 to 85)

Your annual RMD is calculated by taking your total tax-deferred account balances on **December 31 of the prior year** and dividing that number by an IRS "Life Expectancy Factor" found in Table III (the Uniform Lifetime Table). As you age, this factor shrinks, which automatically forces you to withdraw a larger percentage of your remaining balance each year.

| **Account Owner's Age** | **IRS Distribution Factor** | **Equivalent Annual Percentage** |
|---|---|---|
| **73** | 26.5 | 3.77% |
| **74** | 25.5 | 3.92% |
| **75** | 24.6 | 4.07% |
| **76** | 23.7 | 4.22% |
| **77** | 22.9 | 4.37% |
| **78** | 22.0 | 4.55% |
| **79** | 21.1 | 4.74% |

| **Account Owner's Age** | **IRS Distribution Factor** | **Equivalent Annual Percentage** |
|---|---|---|
| **80** | 20.2 | 4.95% |
| **81** | 19.4 | 5.15% |
| **82** | 18.5 | 5.41% |
| **83** | 17.7 | 5.65% |
| **84** | 16.8 | 5.95% |
| **85** | 16.0 | 6.25% |

# Real-World Example: $200,000 Account

## Balance

To see how the shrinking IRS factor changes your mandatory distributions over time, assume you enter your first RMD year with a flat **$200,000 account balance** on December 31 of the previous year.

For the sake of clear comparison, the table below assumes a flat $200,000 base at each age to cleanly illustrate how your age alone increases your mandatory cash-out, independent of market growth or losses.

- **At Age 73:**

$200,000 div 26.5 = $7,547.17 (or 3.77%)

- **At Age 75:**

$200,000 div 24.6 = $8,130.08 (or 4.07%)

- **At Age 80:**

$200,000 div 20.2 = $9,900.99 (or 4.95%)

- **At Age 85:**

$200,000 div 16.0 = $12,500.00 (or 6.25%)

Failing to take your full RMD by the deadline triggers an IRS tax penalty. The SECURE Act 2.0 set this penalty at **25%** of the amount you failed to withdraw, though it drops to **10%** if you correct the mistake and file an updated return within a standard two-year correction window.

As you can see, there are a number of different age milestones that you do not want to miss! Remember to do your own research and dive deeper into each of these milestones. You will find nuances and niches and realize this is general information and your situation may be different. Choose to become a student of retirement!

# Baker's Dozen
## Retiree Regrets

Before we dive into the longer list, I wanted to provide you with this quick snapshot of some of the top regrets from Retirees:

1. Not saving enough/not starting to save sooner
2. Not retiring sooner!
3. Not understanding taxes, penalties and consequences
4. Not having a financial plan or consulting experts
5. Not having a purpose and how time would be used in retirement
6. Not taking care of their health and understanding healthcare choices
7. Not spending enough time on key relationships
8. Unwise spending on big ticket items that depreciate
9. Not involving spouse/partner in the retirement planning
10. Not pursuing passion projects and ideas
11. Not traveling more
12. Not taking advantage of the "Go/Go" years when energy and health were best
13. Not switching from savings to spending mentality and hoarding money in early years of retirement

# Biggest Regret

Overwhelmingly, the single biggest regret among retirees is not saving early enough or putting away enough money for the future. Because this regret is so incredibly common, we are dedicating a full chapter to unpacking it.

Use the data below to see how your own retirement savings stack up against the rest of the country.

The most widely cited source for retirement savings by age is the U.S. Federal Reserve's **Survey of Consumer Finances (SCF)**. One of the key findings is that the **average (mean) retirement balance is much higher than the median** because a relatively small number of households have very large retirement accounts.

## U.S. Retirement Savings by Age (Retirement Accounts Only)

(401(K), 403(B), IRA, KEOGH, AND SIMILAR RETIREMENT ACCOUNTS)

| Age Cohort | Median Retirement Savings | Average Retirement Savings |
|---|---|---|
| **Under 35** | $18,800 | $49,130 |
| **35–44** | $45,000 | $141,520 |
| **45–54** | $115,000 | $313,220 |
| **55–64** | $185,000 | $537,560 |
| **65–74** | $200,000 | $609,230 |
| **75+** | $130,000 | $462,410 |

Source: Federal Reserve Survey of Consumer Finances (2022 data) as compiled and summarized by multiple financial research organizations.

There are numerous methods available to determine whether your nest egg is on track. In analyzing the leading frameworks across the industry, I have uncovered several distinct strategies to calculate your target numbers.

Keep in mind that these are general guidelines—which is precisely why it is so critical to partner with a qualified professional, like a CFP or CPA, and to become a dedicated student of retirement planning yourself. Consider this foundational information a launchpad for your own deeper investigation into what works best for your specific lifestyle.

## Part 1: Age-Based Salary Multipliers

These guidelines use your current age as a fitness check for your savings. They assume you will want to maintain your current standard of living and that you will receive some help from Social Security.

Fidelity Investments suggests the following:

| Age Milestone | Fidelity Guideline | Example Target (for a $100,000 Salary) |
|---|---|---|
| **Age 30** | 1x salary | $100,000 |
| **Age 40** | 3x salary | $300,000 |
| **Age 50** | 6x salary | $500,000 to $600,000 |
| **Age 60** | 8x salary | $800,000 |
| **Age 65 to 67** | 10x to 11x salary (at 67) | $1,000,000 to $1,100,000 |

### The Age 30 Milestone (1x Salary)

- **The Example:** If you earn $50,000 a year when you turn 30, this rule suggests you should have $50,000 saved for retirement.
- **The Explanation:** This is your first major savings checkpoint. It assumes you started working and saving a portion of your income

around age 25. Having one full year of pay tucked away by 30 gives that money plenty of time to grow before you actually stop working.

## The Age 40 Milestone (3x Salary)

- **The Example:** If your salary grows to $80,000 by the time you reach age 40, your target nest egg (total retirement savings) is $240,000.
- **The Explanation:** In your 30s, your career often speeds up and you might earn more money. This rule says your savings need to speed up too. By tripling your annual salary in savings by age 40, you ensure that market growth can start doing the heavy lifting for you.

## The Age 50 Milestone (5x to 6x Salary)

- **The Example:** If you earn $100,000 at age 50, major financial institutions suggest you should have between $500,000 (T. Rowe Price) and $600,000 (Fidelity) saved.
- **The Explanation:** Age 50 is a turning point. You are likely in your peak earning years. This milestone ensures you stay on track. It is also the age where the government lets you make "catch-up contributions," meaning you can legally put extra money into your tax-advantaged retirement accounts each year.

## The Age 60 Milestone (8x Salary)

- **The Example:** If you are making $120,000 a year at age 60, your target savings total is $960,000.
- **The Explanation:** At 60, you are less than a decade away from typical retirement. Your savings account needs to be large because it will soon replace your job. Having eight times your salary means

your investments are robust enough to handle market shifts right before you exit the workforce.

## Age 65 - 67 Milestone (10x to 11x Salary)

- **The Example:** If your final career salary is $100,000, you should aim to cross the retirement finish line with $1 million to $1.1 million.
- **The Explanation:** Age 67 is the Full Retirement Age for Social Security for most modern workers. Top investment companies estimate that if you hit this 10x to 11x multiplier, your portfolio can safely generate roughly 45% of your pre-retirement income. When you combine that with Social Security payments, you can come closer to achieving the lifestyle you want to maintain.

### Advantages

- Easy benchmark at each live stage

### Disadvantages

- Assumes average retirement spending patterns
- Does not account for your actual expenses, lifestyle or health situation

# Part 2: Spending and Income Replacement Methods

These theories do not look at your current age or what you earn today. Instead, they focus entirely on how much money you plan to pull out of your accounts once you stop working.

Here are some of the different retirement methods/rules to consider:

- **4% Rule**
- **The 25x Expense Rule**
- **The 70%-80% Income Replacement Rule**
- **The Early Retirement 30x-33x Rule**
- **The Capital Preservation "interest only" Rule**
- **Expense Based Retirement Rule**
- **Gap Analysis Retirement Rule**
- **Guardrail/Bucket Strategy**
- **Vanguards Dynamic Spending Strategy**
- **The "Safety First" Approach**
- **The IRS Life Expectancy**
- **The Home Equity/Reverse Mortgage Strategy**
- **Die With Zero Strategy**
- **Monte Carlo Simulation & Detailed Retirement Software**

# 4% Rule

## How the 4% Rule Works (The Mechanics)

A common misconception is that you take 4% of your portfolio *every single year*. That is **not** how it works. You only look at your total portfolio balance *once*—on the day you retire. After that, your original portfolio size no longer dictates your annual income; **inflation does.**

## A Detailed Example

Let's say you retire with a **$1,000,000** portfolio comprised of 50% equities and 50% bonds.

- **Year 1:** You calculate 4% of your starting balance.

  $1,000,000 times 0.04 = $40,000

  You withdraw **$40,000** to live on in your first year.

- **Year 2:** The stock market drops, and your portfolio shrinks to $900,000. However, inflation for the year was **3%**. You do *not* calculate 4% of $900,000. Instead, you take your Year 1 dollar amount ($40,000) and increase it by 3%.

  $40,000 times 1.03 = $41,200

  You withdraw **$41,200**, even though your portfolio went down.

- **Year 3:** The market recovers, and inflation is **2%**. You take your Year 2 dollar amount ($41,200) and increase it by 2%.

  $41,200 times 1.02 = $42,024

  You withdraw **$42,024**.

You repeat this process every year, maintaining your exact same purchasing power regardless of whether the stock market is booming or crashing.

# Advantages and Disadvantages

While the 4% rule is an incredibly useful starting point, it has distinct flaws when applied blindly to real-world retirements.

## Advantages

- **Extreme Simplicity:** It provides a crystal-clear target. If you know you need $40,000 a year from your investments, you just multiply that by 25 to know you need a $1,000,000 nest egg.
- **Protects Purchasing Power:** Because your raises are tied directly to the Consumer Price Index (CPI), your lifestyle doesn't suffer when gas or groceries get more expensive.
- **Historically Battle-Tested:** Bengen tested this rule against the worst economic environments in modern history, including the Great Depression and the stagflation of the 1970s. In 100% of historical 30-year windows, a 50/50 portfolio lasted at least 30 years.
- **High Probability of Excess Wealth:** Because the rule is built to survive worst-case scenarios, if you experience an *average* or *good* market, you will likely end your 30-year retirement with significantly more money than you started with.

## Disadvantages

- **The "Sequence of Returns" Vulnerability:** The absolute biggest threat to this rule is the first few years of retirement. If you retire right into a major, prolonged bear market, pulling out inflation-adjusted dollars from a rapidly shrinking pool of assets can cannibalize your portfolio so severely that it may never recover.
- **Inflexible and Unnatural:** Humans don't spend money this way. In the real world, if the market crashes, retirees naturally tighten their belts. If the market booms, they might travel more. The 4% rule assumes you will blindly demand your inflation raise even if your portfolio is bleeding out.

- **Tax Blindness:** The rule deals in gross dollars. It doesn't account for whether your money is coming from a taxable brokerage account, a tax-free Roth, or a tax-deferred traditional IRA where Uncle Sam will claim a massive percentage of your withdrawal.
- **The "Leftover Wealth" Problem:** Because it is designed for worst-case historical data, it is heavily conservative. In roughly 80% of historical scenarios, retirees using the 4% rule finished 30 years with their initial principal completely intact or significantly multiplied—meaning they may have needlessly deprived themselves of experiences or spending early in retirement.

# The 25x Expense Rule

The **25x expense rule** is a quick-calculation framework used to determine your "Financial Independence" number—the total amount of capital you need to have saved before you can safely retire.

It is the mathematical twin of the **4% rule**. Because dividing a number by 4% (0.04) is mathematically identical to multiplying it by 25, the 25x rule looks at the exact same coin from the opposite side. While the 4% rule tells you how much you can *take out* in retirement, the 25x rule tells you how much you must *accumulate* before you start.

## How It Works (The Mechanics)

The formula itself is deceptively simple:

Target Nest Egg = Estimated Annual Expenses to be Funded by the Portfolio times 25

The most critical mistake people make when applying this rule is multiplying their *total* retirement budget by 25. To use the rule accurately, you must first subtract any guaranteed, non-portfolio income sources—such as Social Security, a pension, or rental income—to isolate the exact amount your investments are responsible for generating.

## A Detailed Example

Let's look at a couple mapping out their retirement target.

### Step 1: Isolate the Net Portfolio Demand

- **Total Annual Retirement Budget:** $100,000 (including taxes, healthcare, and lifestyle spending).
- **Projected Social Security Income:** $40,000 per year combined.
- **Net Portfolio Demand:**

  $100,000 - $40,000 = $60,000

  The investments must provide **$60,000** per year.

### Step 2: Apply the 25x Multiplier

To find their target nest egg, they multiply that net portfolio demand by 25:

$60,000 times 25 = $1,500,000

According to the rule, once their combined investment accounts (IRAs, 401(k)s, brokerage accounts) reach **$1,500,000**, they have hit their target. If they withdraw 4% of that $1,500,000 in Year 1 ($60,000) and adjust that dollar amount for inflation every year after, historical data suggests the portfolio has a near-100% chance of lasting at least 30 years.

# Advantages and Disadvantages

## Advantages

- **Instant Back-of-the-Napkin Math:** It eliminates complexity during the early and mid-stages of retirement planning. It gives you an immediate, tangible goal to aim for without needing complex financial software.
- **Clear Savings Milestones:** It allows savers to track their progress in fractions. For instance, if your target multiplier is 25x, reaching 5x, 10x, or 15x of your annual expenses provides clear psychological benchmarks on the path to retirement.
- **Grounded in Historical Safety:** Because it is built directly on William Bengen's landmark 1994 "clean canvas" data, it carries a built-in safety margin designed to survive severe historical market crashes, including the Great Depression and the stagflation of the 1970s.

## Disadvantages

- **The 30-Year Horizon Constraint:** The 25x multiplier is strictly calibrated for a standard **30-year retirement window**.
- If you retire early (e.g., at age 50 or 55) and need the money to last 40 or 50 years, a 25x multiplier is often too risky; early retirees

frequently use a **30x or 33x multiplier** (equivalent to a 3% or 3.3% withdrawal rate).

- Conversely, if you retire at age 70, a 25x multiplier may cause you to over-save and needlessly delay retirement.

- **The "Tax Blindness" Vulnerability:** The rule treats all dollars as equal. If your $1,500,000 nest egg sits entirely inside a traditional, tax-deferred IRA, every dollar you withdraw will be taxed as ordinary income. If you need a *net* $60,000 to pay your bills, you might actually have to withdraw $72,000 to cover the tax drag—meaning your true accumulation goal should have been based on $72,000 ($1.8 million), not $60,000.

- **Assumes Linear Spending:** The 25x rule assumes your real spending stays perfectly flat (adjusted only for inflation) for three decades. In reality, retirement spending is typically a "smile" curve: high in the active early years (travel, hobbies), dipping in the middle years, and spiking at the end due to healthcare and long-term care costs.

- **Sequence of Returns Risk at the Starting Line:** The rule assumes average historical market recoveries. If you hit your 25x number and retire precisely at the peak of a market bubble right before a prolonged multi-year bear market, the rigidity of the model can place the portfolio under severe early stress.

# The 70% to 80% Income Replacement Rule

The **income replacement rule** (often called the replacement ratio) is the traditional benchmark used by the financial services industry to estimate your retirement needs.

Instead of building a budget from scratch, this rule operates on a simple premise: your retirement lifestyle will be directly anchored to whatever you were earning right before you stopped working. The standard rule of thumb dictates that you will need **70% to 80% of your pre-retirement gross income** to maintain your standard of living once you clock out for the last time.

## How It Works (The Mechanics)

The rule assumes that your expenses will naturally drop when you retire, meaning you don't need a full 100% of your former salary.

## Why the target is lower than 100%:

- **No more retirement saving:** You are no longer funnelling 10% to 15% of your pay check into 401(k)s or IRAs. You are now spending down assets, not building them.
- **Lower payroll taxes:** You no longer pay the 7.65% FICA tax (Social Security and Medicare) on earned income.
- **Work expenses disappear:** Commuting costs, professional wardrobes, lunches out, and dry cleaning drop to zero.
- **Debt is often gone:** Many retirees aim to have their primary mortgage paid off by the time they retire, eliminating their largest monthly cash outflow.

## A Detailed Example

Let's look at a corporate manager earning a gross salary of **$130,000** a year.

**Step 1: Calculate the Replacement Target**

Using the standard 80% replacement baseline, we calculate their annual retirement income goal:

$130,000 times 0.80 = $104,000

The target is **$104,000** per year.

**Step 2: Factor in Guaranteed Income**

Next, they layer in non-portfolio income. Let's assume their projected Social Security benefit at their target retirement age is **$34,000** a year.

$104,000 - $34,000 = $70,000

Their investments are on the hook to generate a **$70,000** annual stream.

**Step 3: Determine the Required Nest Egg**

To find the final savings goal, they apply the 4% rule (multiplying the portfolio gap by 25):

$70,000 times 25 = $1,750,000

According to the income replacement model, this individual needs a **$1,750,000** nest egg to safely retire.

# Advantages and Disadvantages

While this rule has been the default setting for financial calculators for decades, it is a blunt instrument that works beautifully for some and fails miserably for others.

**Advantages**

- **Low Friction/High Simplicity:** It requires almost no homework. You don't need to track down gas receipts or grocery bills; you just need to look at your current W-2 or tax return.

- **Perfect for Early-Career Planning:** If you are 35 or 45 years old, trying to guess what a gallon of milk or health insurance will cost in twenty years is impossible. This rule gives you a highly functional, scalable target to aim for during your peak accumulation years.

- **Focuses on Income, Not Just Net Worth:** It correctly shifts the conversation away from accumulating a random "million-dollar lump sum" and focuses on replicating a steady, sustainable monthly cash flow.

Disadvantages

- **The "Super Saver" Paradox:** This rule actively penalizes people with high savings rates. If you earn $150,000 but live frugally and save 35% of your income ($52,500), you are actually only living on $97,500. If a planner blindly applies the 80% rule to your $150,000 salary, they will tell you that you need $120,000 a year in retirement—forcing you to over-save for a lifestyle you never actually lived.

- **Fatally Flawed for Early Retirement:** If you intend to retire early, your mortgage might not be paid off yet, and you will have to bridge a massive gap in healthcare coverage before Medicare kicks in at age 65. The income replacement rule completely misses these lumpy, age-dependent cost spikes.

- **Tax Structural Blindness:** It uses gross (pre-tax) income as its baseline. However, your retirement tax brackets can look completely different depending on whether your income streams flow from tax-deferred Traditional IRAs, tax-free Roth accounts, or capital-gains-taxed brokerage accounts.

# The "Early Retirement" 30x to 33x Rule

The **30x to 33x expense rule** is the conservative, ultra-safe sibling of the traditional 25x rule. It is a framework popularized by the early retirement and FIRE (Financial Independence, Retire Early) movements.

The rule is designed to solve one massive problem: **longevity risk**. While a traditional retirement timeline only needs a portfolio to survive for 25 to 30 years, an early retirement (retiring in your 40s or 50s) requires a portfolio to sustain you for 40, 50, or even 60 years.

To survive a half-century without working, you need a bigger safety margin.

## How the Rule Works (The Mechanics)

The core math is simple. Instead of accumulating 25 times your annual net expenses, you accumulate 30 to 33 times that amount.

Mathematically, changing the multiplier changes your **Safe Withdrawal Rate (SWR)**. The multiplier is simply the inverse of your withdrawal rate:

- **25x Expenses = 4.0% Withdrawal Rate** (Standard 30-year horizon)
- **30x Expenses = 3.33% Withdrawal Rate** (Extended 35 to 40-year horizon)
- **33x Expenses = 3.03% Withdrawal Rate** (Ultra-long 40 to 50+ year horizon)

By lowering your initial withdrawal rate to roughly 3%, you drastically lower the risk that a poorly timed market crash at the beginning of your retirement will permanently bankrupt your portfolio.

| Retirement Style | Target Age | Portfolio Multiplier | Safe Withdrawal Rate (SWR) | Target Horizon |
|---|---|---|---|---|
| **Early / FIRE** | 40–55 | **30x to 33x** | 3.0% - 3.33% | 40–50+ Years |
| **Traditional** | 62–65 | **25x** | 4.0% | 30 Years |
| **Late-Stage** | 70+ | **20x to 22x** | 4.5% - 5.0% | 15–22 Years |

## A Detailed Early Retirement Example

Imagine an individual who wants to leave corporate life at **age 48**. They expect to live to age 93, meaning their portfolio must last an absolute minimum of **45 years**.

After calculating their baseline spending, factoring in independent healthcare premiums before Medicare kicks in, and subtracting a small projected real estate income stream, they determine their portfolio needs to provide a net income of **$70,000** per year.

### The Traditional 25x Calculation (Too Risky)

$70,000 times 25 = $1,750,000 Nest Egg

If they retire at 48 with $1.75 million and pull out 4%, historical rolling periods show a roughly 15% to 20% chance that they will run out of money before age 93, because 4% was never stress-tested for a 45-year window.

### The 33x Early Retirement Calculation

$70,000 times 33 = $2,310,000 Nest Egg

By working a bit longer to accumulate $2.31 million, their starting withdrawal drops to a microscopic 3.03% ($70,000 div $2,310,000).

At a 3% withdrawal rate, the portfolio's historical success rate over a 50-year period climbs to **virtually 100%**. Even if they live through a repeat of the 1930s Great Depression or 1970s stagflation right at the start of their early retirement, the portfolio generates enough compounding growth on the remaining $2.31 million to protect the core principal.

# Advantages and Disadvantages

## Advantages

- **Defeats Sequence of Returns Risk:** Over a 50-year horizon, you are statistically guaranteed to live through multiple recessions, market bubbles, and bear markets. A 3% withdrawal rate (33x) is small enough that you can leave your growth assets untouched during market corrections.

- **Absorbs the "Pre-Medicare" Healthcare Shock:** Retiring early means paying for private health insurance or managing your income precisely to qualify for ACA subsidies for up to 15+ years before Medicare triggers at age 65. The extra padding in a 33x multiplier gives you the capital needed to absorb shifting insurance premiums.

- **Compensates for Social Security Delays:** If you retire at 48, your Social Security benefit calculation will include a dozen "$0 earnings" years, shrinking your eventual check. Furthermore, you can't touch that money for nearly two decades. The 33x multiplier assumes your portfolio does 100% of the heavy lifting for the first half of your retirement.

## Disadvantages

- **The "One More Year" Trap:** Moving your target from 25x to 33x expenses requires a massive amount of extra savings. If you spend $70,000 a year, that is an extra $560,000 you have to accumulate. This can lead to severe burnout, forcing people to stay at jobs they dislike for an extra 3 to 5 years just to hit a hyper-conservative mathematical metric.
- **Massive Leftover Wealth (Over-Saving):** Because a 3% withdrawal rate is so conservative, if the market experiences even *average* historical returns, your portfolio will grow exponentially over 40 years. It is highly likely that an early retiree using the 33x rule will die with significantly more millions than they started with—meaning they traded precious youth and time working when they didn't actually need to.
- **The Age 59½ Accessibility Hurdle:** Accumulating 33x expenses is great, but if 90% of that money is locked up in traditional tax-deferred 401(k)s or IRAs, accessing it before age 59½ without triggering the IRS 10% early withdrawal penalty requires complex structural planning (such as Roth Conversion Ladders or SEPP/Rule 72(t) distributions).

# The Capital Preservation "Interest-Only" Method

The **Capital Preservation "Interest-Only" Method** (often called the yield-only strategy) is a retirement income blueprint based on a classic financial mantra: **Live off the golden eggs, but never kill the golden goose.**

Unlike total-return strategies like the 4% rule, which systematically consume both your principal and your earnings over a 30-year period, the interest-only method relies entirely on the passive cash flow generated by your portfolio—such as bond coupons, stock dividends, and interest from liquid cash vehicles. You completely lock away the core principal, vowed never to sell a single share or contract to fund your lifestyle.

## How It Works (The Mechanics)

To make this method work, a retiree shifts their asset location and allocation toward vehicles focused primarily on current yield rather than aggressive price appreciation. This includes a blend of U.S. Treasuries, certificates of deposit (CDs), dividend aristocrat equities, Real Estate Investment Trusts (REITs), and corporate fixed income.

Instead of setting a fixed spending target and withdrawing it mechanically, your annual lifestyle spending budget is dictated entirely by whatever yield your portfolio happens to spin off each year.

## A Detailed Example

Let's look at a retiree who has accumulated a **$1,500,000** portfolio. To protect the principal while securing a reliable cash flow, they build a diversified, income-producing portfolio matching the current yield environment:

- **Fixed Income Bucket ($750,000):** Invested in a ladder of U.S. Treasuries and high-yield CDs generating an average yield of **4.5%**.
- **Dividend Equity Bucket ($750,000):** Invested in a mix of dividend growth ETFs and high-quality blue-chip stocks averaging a **3.5%** dividend yield.

### The Math:

- **Fixed Income Yield:** $750,000 times 0.045 = $33,750
- **Dividend Equity Yield:** $750,000 times 0.035 = $26,250
- **Total Annual Portfolio Income: $60,000**
- **Blended Portfolio Yield: 4.0%**

Every month or quarter, the brokerage account sweeps these automated dividend and interest payments directly into the Retiree's checking account, functioning exactly like a corporate pay check.

If this retiree also receives **$35,000** a year from Social Security, their total annual gross income is **$95,000**. At the end of year one, year ten, and year thirty, the underlying **$1,500,000 core principal remains 100% intact**.

## Advantages and Disadvantages

While this is the ultimate "sleep-at-night" strategy for a specific type of investor, it creates structural blind spots that can quietly erode a retirement plan if left unmanaged.

### Advantages

- **Zero Sequence of Returns Risk:** This is the strategy's superpower. If the stock market crashes by 30% right after you retire, you don't care. Because you never liquidate shares to pay for groceries, you never "lock in" paper losses. As long as the companies keep paying their dividends and the bonds pay their coupons, your income stream remains stable while your principal waits out the market recovery.

- **An Absolute Shield Against Longevity Risk:** You cannot mathematically outlive your money because you aren't actually spending your money—only the rent your money charges the market. The timeline of your retirement could stretch for 30, 50, or 70 years, and the portfolio will survive.

- **Perfect for Legacy and Estate Planning:** If your primary financial goal is to pass down significant, multi-generational wealth to children, grandchildren, or charitable foundations, this method guarantees they inherit the exact nest egg you spent a lifetime building.

## Disadvantages

- **The Silent Inflation Trap:** If you pull out a flat $60,000 every single year to live on, inflation will relentlessly chew away at your purchasing power. An item costing $1,000 at the start of a 30-year retirement can easily cost over $2,000 by the end. Unless your assets feature a built-in growth mechanism (like dividend-growth stocks that increase payouts annually), your standard of living will steadily decline.

- **Severe Reinvestment and Interest Rate Risk:** Fixed income yields are tied directly to current macroeconomic climates. If you lock up money in 4.5% CDs and Treasuries, but interest rates drop significantly over the next decade, your income will plunge when those vehicles mature and you are forced to reinvest the principal at much lower prevailing rates.

- **A Massive Capital Barrier to Entry:** Because you cannot tap the principal, you need a much larger pool of wealth to achieve the same initial standard of living as someone using a total-return strategy. Pulling a safe $60,000 a year out of an interest-only strategy requires a massive, unencumbered lump sum, whereas a total-return drawdown can deliver the same income from a much leaner base by intentionally consuming principal over time.

# Expense-Based Retirement Planning

**Expense-based retirement planning** is the practice of building a retirement strategy around a detailed, line-item projection of your actual future spending, rather than relying on broad shortcuts.

It stands in direct contrast to the traditional **Income Replacement Method**, which lazily assumes you will automatically need 70% to 80% of whatever your salary happens to be when you finish working. Instead of guessing based on what you *make*, expense-based planning focuses entirely on what you actually *spend*.

## How It Works

The strategy breaks your retirement timeline into distinct spending buckets, separates your needs from your wants, and isolates the exact amount your portfolio needs to produce. The process follows a simple formula:

1. **Audit Current Spending:** Analyze 12 months of bank and credit card statements to establish a real-world baseline.
2. **Adjust for the "Retirement Reality":** Strip out expenses that disappear (payroll taxes, 401(k)/IRA contributions, commuting, or a paid-off mortgage) and add new ones (independent healthcare premiums, increased travel, or hobbies).
3. **Categorize Into Core vs. Discretionary:**
    - **Essential (Fixed):** Housing, healthcare, utilities, insurance, food.
    - **Discretionary (Variable):** Travel, dining out, entertainment, gifting.

4. **Calculate the Portfolio Gap:** Subtract guaranteed income sources (Social Security, pensions, annuities) from your total retirement expenses. The remaining amount is your **Portfolio Gap**—the actual number your investments must safely fund.

# A Detailed Example

Let's look at a case study comparing a standard income-replacement calculation against a detailed expense-based approach.

Imagine a couple earning **$150,000** a year before retirement. They expect a combined **$35,000** annually from Social Security at full retirement age.

## The Income Replacement Shortcut

Using the standard 80% rule of thumb, a planner tells them they need **$120,000** per year.

- Subtracting their $35,000 Social Security leaves a **$85,000** portfolio gap.
- Using the 4% rule, they are told they need a nest egg of **$2,125,000** ($85,000 × 25).

## The Expense-Based Reality

The couple sits down and maps out their actual anticipated line items:

- **Essential Annual Costs:** $48,000 (Property taxes, insurance, utilities, groceries, and premium healthcare coverage).
- **Discretionary Annual Costs:** $24,000 (Heavy travel during their early "Go-Go" years, dining out, and hobbies).
- **Total Real Outflow: $72,000** per year.

Now the math changes completely:

- Subtracting their $35,000 Social Security leaves an actual **$37,000** portfolio gap.
- Using the exact same 4% rule, their true required nest egg is **$925,000** ($37,000 × 25).

By focusing on real expenses rather than a generalized income ratio, they discover they can safely retire with over $1.1 million *less* than the standard rule of thumb suggested.

# Advantages and Disadvantages

## Advantages

- **Prevents "One-Size-Fits-None" Over-Saving:** As shown above, rule-of-thumb replacement ratios often force people to work years longer than necessary to hit a savings goal they don't actually need.
- **Granular Tax and Subsidy Engineering:** Knowing your exact spending requirement allows you to control your tax brackets precisely. It helps you manage your Modified Adjusted Gross Income (MAGI) to optimize for early retirement incentives like Affordable Care Act (ACA) premium subsidies.
- **Enables Phase-Based Adjustments:** Spending isn't linear. An expense-based model allows you to plan for higher lifestyle spending in your active "Go-Go" years (ages 60-70), which naturally tapers off into your "Slow-Go" years (ages 70-80).

## Disadvantages

- **High Upfront Effort:** It requires a tedious review of real data. You cannot guess; you have to physically account for lumpy expenses like roof replacements, new cars, and rising property insurance premiums.

- **The Healthcare Wildcard:** While grocery bills are predictable, out-of-pocket medical costs and long-term care needs decades into the future are incredibly difficult to project accurately.

- **Asymmetric Inflation:** Different expense categories inflate at different speeds. While your fixed mortgage payment might stay flat or disappear, your healthcare and energy costs can outpace general CPI inflation, threatening a static budget.

# Gap Analysis Method

**Gap analysis retirement planning** is a financial diagnostic framework. While expense-based planning tells you what your retirement will *cost*, a gap analysis compares that cost against your current trajectory to pinpoint exactly where you stand.

Think of it as a financial GPS: it calculates the distance between your destination (your target retirement lifestyle) and your current location (your projected savings and income), highlighting the exact shortfall—the "gap"—you need to bridge before you cross the finish line.

## How It Works

A gap analysis doesn't just look at a single number. It evaluates two distinct types of gaps:

1. **The Income Gap (Annual):** The difference between your annual retirement spending target and your guaranteed income sources (like Social Security or a pension). This is the amount your portfolio must generate each year.
2. **The Capital Gap (Lump Sum):** The difference between the nest egg size required to fund that Income Gap safely and what your current savings are actually projected to grow to by your target retirement date.

The process typically moves through four clean phases:

- **Establish the Target:** Pinpoint the annual retirement lifestyle cost.
- **Layer in Guarantees:** Subtract non-portfolio income sources.
- **Project Current Trajectory:** Calculate what your existing accounts will be worth at retirement based on your current savings rate and a conservative growth estimate.
- **Quantify the Shortfall:** Subtract the projected nest egg from the required nest egg to find your Capital Gap.

# A Detailed Example

Let's look at a couple, both age 57, who want to retire in 5 years at age 62.

## Phase 1 & 2: Finding the Income Gap

- **Target Annual Expenses:** $90,000
- **Projected Social Security (Combined at 62):** $40,000
- **Annual Income Gap: $50,000** (This is what the portfolio must supply)

## Phase 3: The Target Nest Egg vs. Reality

Using a safe withdrawal rate of 4%, they divide their $50,000 Income Gap by 0.04 to find their required nest egg.

- **Required Nest Egg: $1,250,000**

Next, they look at their current reality. They currently have $750,000 saved and are contributing $15,000 a year. Assuming a conservative 6% annual growth rate over the next 5 years, their portfolio is on track to reach $1,090,000 by the time they hit age 62.

- **Projected Nest Egg at Age 62: $1,090,000**

## Phase 4: The Capital Gap

Now they subtract their projected reality from their target:

| | |
|---|---|
| Required Nest Egg goal | = $1,250,000 |
| Projected Nest Egg (current path) | = $1,090,000 |
| The Capital Gap | =$160,000 |

## Closing the Gap

Because they ran this analysis *before* retiring, they have a clear metric to solve for. To close that $160,000 gap over the next 5 years, they can choose from a few specific levers:

- **Save more:** Increase their annual savings from $15,000 to roughly $43,000 for the next 5 years.
- **Work longer:** Delay retirement from age 62 to 64. This gives their current money two more years to grow, adds two more years of contributions, and increases their permanent Social Security benefit (which shrinks the Income Gap entirely).
- **Downsize expectations:** Reduce their target retirement spending by roughly $6,400 a year to match the $1,090,000 portfolio they are on track to have.

# Advantages and Disadvantages

## Advantages

- **Highly Actionable Insights:** Instead of a vague feeling of "I hope I have enough," it gives you a precise dollar figure to solve for while you still have time to make adjustments.
- **Isolates the True Variables:** It forces you to look at your retirement date, savings rate, and spending goals as interlocking gears. If you turn one gear, you instantly see how it moves the others.
- **Great for Early Warning:** Running a gap analysis 5 to 10 years before your target retirement date gives you an invaluable runway to fix structural shortfalls without disrupting your primary lifestyle goals.

## Disadvantages

- **Hyper-Sensitive to Assumptions:** The entire analysis hinges on estimates for investment growth, inflation, and life expectancy. If you assume a rosy 8% market return but get a flat 3% sequence of returns early on, the gap analysis will give you a false sense of security.
- **Static Nature:** A traditional gap analysis is a snapshot in time. It assumes smooth, linear progress and struggles to naturally account for highly volatile market years or lumpy, unpredictable real-world expenses.
- **Psychological Friction:** Seeing a massive "Capital Gap" printed out on paper can intimidate people into a state of analysis paralysis, causing them to abandon planning altogether rather than making small, incremental adjustments to close it.

# Guardrail/Bucket Strategy

Here is how these two concepts work together.

## The Bucket Strategy (Where the Money Lives)

The bucket strategy is a structural asset allocation framework. It splits your total portfolio into three distinct "buckets" based on *when* you will need to spend the cash. This is designed to prevent you from being forced to sell equities during a market downturn.

- **Bucket 1 (Short-Term / Cash):** Holds 1 to 3 years of living expenses in ultra-safe, liquid vehicles (checking, high-yield savings, CDs).

- **Bucket 2 (Medium-Term / Income):** Holds 3 to 7 years of expenses in stable, income-producing assets (short/intermediate bonds, dividend stocks).

- **Bucket 3 (Long-Term / Growth):** Holds the remainder in diversified equities for long-term growth to combat inflation.

## The Guardrail Method (How Much You Can Safely Spend)

Invented by financial planner Jonathan Guyton and computer scientist William Klinger, the **Guyton-Klinger Guardrails** are dynamic spending rules. Instead of blindly adjusting your initial withdrawal rate for inflation every year (like the classic 4% rule), you monitor your portfolio's performance and adjust your spending up or down based on specific triggers.

The two main rules are:

- **The Capital Preservation Rule (The Upper Guardrail):** If the market crashes and your current withdrawal rate spikes by more than 20% of your initial rate (because your portfolio shrank), you **cut your spending by 10%** to protect the principal.

- **The Prosperity Rule (The Lower Guardrail):** If the market booms and your current withdrawal rate drops by more than 20% of your initial rate (because your portfolio grew so much), you **increase your spending by 10%** to enjoy your wealth.

## How to Combine Them: The "Hybrid" Approach

When you overlay Guardrails onto a Bucket system, you get a highly resilient retirement engine. The buckets provide the behavioral security, while the guardrails provide the math-based rules for refilling those buckets.

Here is exactly how they interact in practice:

### Handling a Bull Market

When Bucket 3 (Equities) is growing rapidly, your overall portfolio value increases, which triggers the **Prosperity Rule**. You can safely increase your annual spending limit. You use the gains from Bucket 3 to top off Bucket 1 (Cash) and Bucket 2 (Fixed Income), ensuring your near-term cash reserves are completely secure while enjoying a little extra lifestyle spending.

### Handling a Bear Market

If the stock market drops significantly, you immediately stop pulling money from Bucket 3. Instead, you live entirely off Bucket 1 (Cash). However, because your total portfolio value has shrunk, your withdrawal rate relative to your current portfolio size has gone up.

If it hits the upper guardrail, the **Capital Preservation Rule** kicks in, and you reduce your annual distribution by 10%. Because you are spending 10% less, your Bucket 1 cash reserves will last even longer, giving Bucket 3 plenty of time to recover without you ever having to sell a single share of stock at a loss.

# The Advantages

## 1. It Solves the Bucket Strategy's Biggest Flaw

A classic Bucket Strategy is great at telling you *where* to put your money, but it is notoriously vague about **when and how to refill the cash buckets**. If the market is choppy for three years, do you refill Bucket 1 from Bucket 2? Do you cannibalize equities while they are down? The Guardrail Method fixes this. It provides the exact mathematical rules for when to harvest gains from your growth bucket (the Prosperity Rule) to top off your cash reserves, and exactly when to freeze refills and cut spending (the Capital Preservation Rule).

## 2. Behavioral Armor against Panic Selling

During a severe market crash, a spread sheets-only approach like the 4% rule asks you to have nerves of steel while watching a single unified portfolio bleed out. The hybrid approach gives you **psychological insulation**. You can physically see that you have 2 to 3 years of cash completely locked down in Bucket 1. Knowing your day-to-day life is safe for the near term prevents you from making the ultimate retirement mistake: panic-selling equities at the bottom of a bear market.

## 3. Permits a Higher Initial Withdrawal Rate

Because you have a built-in agreement with yourself to cut your spending by 10% if a worst-case market crash hits your upper guardrail, you don't have to be as hyper-conservative at the starting line. While a rigid retirement plan might force you to stick to a tight 4% initial withdrawal, a hybrid guardrail strategy safely allows you to start at **4.5% or even 5.0%**, because the system features a built-in relief valve.

## 4. Maximizes "Health-Span" Spending

By utilizing the **Prosperity Rule (lower guardrail)**, the system forces you to take a raise when the market booms. This prevents the common tragedy of retirees over-saving and hoarding wealth into their late 70s and 80s when their physical ability to travel, explore, and enjoy that money has naturally declined.

# The Disadvantages

## 1. High Operational Complexity and Maintenance

This strategy is a logistical commitment. Every year, you have to:

- Re-calculate your current withdrawal rate based on your fluctuating total portfolio value.
- Check your proximity to both the upper and lower guardrail thresholds.
- Manually execute the transfers to rebalance assets from Bucket 3 down to Bucket 2 and Bucket 1. If you manage your own investments, this requires meticulous record-keeping. If you hire an advisor to do it, the management fees can chew into your returns.

## 2. The Drag of "Cash Drag"

To keep Bucket 1 (Cash) and Bucket 2 (Income/Short-term bonds) fully operational, a significant percentage of your net worth—often 5 to 7 years' worth of living expenses—is intentionally kept out of the stock market. Over a 30-year retirement, this massive safety buffer creates **cash drag**, meaning your total portfolio will almost certainly underperform a simple, unified 60/40 or 70/30 stock-and-bond portfolio. You are sacrificing total lifetime wealth in exchange for near-term stability

## 3. Tax Efficiency Friction

Moving money between buckets to fulfil guardrail rules can trigger a logistical tax nightmare if your assets aren't housed in the right places. For example, if your Growth Bucket (Bucket 3) is sitting in a taxable brokerage account, selling off appreciated equities during a boom year to refill your Cash Bucket will trigger significant **capital gains taxes**. Conversely, if you pull extra money out of a traditional IRA to satisfy a prosperity adjustment, you could inadvertently push yourself into a higher ordinary income tax bracket or trigger stealth Medicare premium surcharges (IRMAA).

## 4. The Pain of Mandatory Cuts

The math behind the Capital Preservation Rule is unemotional. If the market drops severely enough to trigger the upper guardrail, you *must* cut your portfolio distributions by 10%. If your retirement budget is already lean, or if inflation is driving up the cost of groceries and utilities at the exact same time the market is crashing, forcing a 10% lifestyle cut can cause genuine financial and psychological strain.

**The Takeaway:** The Bucket Strategy gives you the *liquidity buffer* to survive a down market without panic selling, while the Guardrail Method gives you the exact *mathematical triggers* to know when to tighten your belt or when it's safe to spend more.

# Die With Zero Method

The **"Die with Zero" method**, popularized by author and energy trader Bill Perkins in his book *Die with Zero*, is a radical departure from traditional retirement planning.

While traditional models (like the 4% rule or Capital Preservation) focus on accumulating as much money as possible to ensure you never run out, the "Die with Zero" philosophy argues that **dying with a large nest egg represents a tragic waste of your life energy.**

Perkins argues that money is simply a tool to buy life experiences. If you die with $500,000 left in your bank account, that represents years of your youth spent working, stressing, and saving for experiences you never actually had. The goal of this method is to perfectly optimize your life enjoyment by sliding your net worth down to zero precisely on the day you pass away.

## The Core Mechanics

The strategy is built on several unique financial and psychological concepts:

1. **Memory Dividends:** When you pay for an experience early in life (like a trip or a hobby), it doesn't just happen once. It pays "dividends" for the rest of your life every time you reminisce about it, share stories, or look at photos. Therefore, spending money on experiences earlier in retirement yields higher lifetime returns than waiting until you are older.

2. **Time Bucketing:** Instead of a generic bucket list, you divide your future into distinct age blocks (e.g., ages 60–65, 65–70, 70–75). You then assign experiences to the bucket where you will have the physical health to actually enjoy them (e.g., backpacking Europe at 62 vs. going on a cruise at 82).

3. **The Net Worth Peak:** Traditional planning assumes your wealth should keep growing until you stop working, and then hover flat. "Die with Zero" requires you to find your "peak" wealth point—usually in your late 50s or early 60s—where you intentionally

begin spending *more* than your portfolio generates, deliberately drawing down the principal.

4. **Targeted Giving (Giving Early):** If you want to leave money to children or charity, this rule says doing so at your death is highly inefficient. If you die at 85, your children will likely be 55 or 60—already established and past the age where an inheritance would make the biggest structural impact on their lives. The method advocates giving your children their inheritance while they are between the ages of 26 and 35, when it can help them buy a house or start a business.

# A Detailed Example

Let's compare a traditional retiree with a "Die with Zero" retiree. Both retire at age 62 with a **$1,500,000** portfolio.

## The Traditional Path

The traditional retiree uses a conservative total-return strategy, withdrawing a flat $60,000 a year. Out of fear of the unknown, they turn down expensive trips, delay buying a camper van, and keep a strict budget. They live to age 86. Because the stock market performed reasonably well over those 24 years, their portfolio actually grew. They die with **$1.2 million** left over. Their children inherit the money in their late 50s.

## The "Die with Zero" Path

The "Die with Zero" retiree maps out their plan dynamically:

- **Ages 62–67 (The active "Go-Go" years):** They deliberately spend $95,000 a year, dipping heavily into principal. They fund major family vacations, travel actively, and optimize their health-span.
- **Age 68:** They isolate $200,000 and distribute it to their children *now*, helping them with down payments on their first homes.
- **Ages 68–78:** Their spending naturally slows down as physical mobility tapers. They spend $55,000 a year.

- **Age 78+:** To protect against the risk of living to 100 and running completely out of money, they use a portion of their remaining asset base to purchase a guaranteed Single Premium Immediate Annuity (SPIA) and long-term care insurance. This completely offloads their longevity risk to an insurance company, giving them a guaranteed income floor until death, allowing them to safely spend down their last remaining discretionary dollars to zero.

# Advantages and Disadvantages

## Advantages

- **Maximizes Lifetime Fulfillment:** It shifts the metric of a "successful retirement" away from your final bank account balance and focuses entirely on maximizing your total lifetime fulfillment.
- **Aligns Spending with Health-Span:** It acknowledges the harsh biological reality that your ability to enjoy wealth declines as you age. It encourages you to spend money when you have the health to enjoy it, rather than hoarding wealth for your 80s when your physical world naturally shrinks.
- **Highly Efficient Generosity:** It allows you to watch your children or grandchildren enjoy their inheritance while you are still alive to see the impact of your hard work.

## Disadvantages

- **Extreme Longevity and Timing Risk:** The absolute hardest part of this method is that nobody knows their exact expiration date. If you plan to hit zero at age 85, but medical advancements help you live to 98, you face catastrophic poverty in your final years unless you have bulletproof income guarantees in place.
- **The Healthcare and Long-Term Care Wildcard:** Assisted living, private memory care, and late-stage medical expenses can be staggering and highly unpredictable. Drawing your net worth down aggressively early in retirement can leave you deeply

vulnerable to medical inflation if you do not pay heavily for long-term care policies.

- **Severe Psychological Resistance:** After spending 30 to 40 years training your brain to save money, invest wisely, and protect your capital, it is incredibly difficult psychologically to intentionally watch your net worth drop year after year.

- **Requires Complex Financial Orchestration:** You cannot just wing this strategy. It requires a precise coordination of personal assets, annuity products, and insurance guardrails to ensure that your essential living expenses remain funded even if your liquid net worth hits zero.

# Vanguard's Dynamic Spending Strategy (Ceiling and Floor Method)

## Explanation

This strategy blends the absolute consistency of the standard 4% rule (dollar-plus-inflation) with the adaptive nature of a fixed-percentage withdrawal. You calculate each year's "target" spending by multiplying a fixed percentage (e.g., 4%) by the *previous year's ending portfolio balance.*

To prevent wild swings in your standard of living, you apply **guardrails**: a maximum "ceiling" and a minimum "floor" based on what you spent the previous year (adjusted for current inflation).

- If the market booms and your target withdrawal exceeds the ceiling, you only take the ceiling amount (leaving the excess in the portfolio to grow).
- If the market crashes and your target withdrawal falls below the floor, you take the floor amount (protecting your lifestyle from a sudden income drop).

## Detailed Example

- **Baseline Setup:** You have a $1,000,000 portfolio, select a **4% baseline rate**, a **5% ceiling**, and a **-2.5% floor**.
- **Year 1:** You withdraw $40,000 ($1,000,000 × 4%).
- **Year 2 Parameters:** Assume inflation is 3%. Your prior year's real spending target adjusts to **$41,200** ($40,000 × 1.03).
    - Your **Ceiling** (+5%): $41,200 × 1.05 = **$43,260**
    - Your **Floor** (-2.5%): $41,200 × 0.975 = **$40,170**

- **The Market Scenario:** Imagine the market experienced a massive bull run, pushing your portfolio up to $1,150,000 by year-end. Your raw 4% target for Year 2 would be $46,000 ($1,150,000 × 0.04).
- **The Outcome:** Because $46,000 is higher than your ceiling ($43,260), your actual Year 2 withdrawal is capped at **$43,260**. The remaining money stays in your account to shield you from future downturns.

## Advantages & Disadvantages

- **Advantages:** Drastically reduces sequence of returns risk (the risk of a market crash early in retirement) and lowers the mathematical probability of running out of money to near zero. It gives you a highly predictable income band.
- **Disadvantages:** Requires manual tracking and calculation every single year. It also prevents you from fully capitalizing on massive bull markets for short-term discretionary spending.

# The "Safety-First" Approach (Wade Pfau / Floor-and-Upside)

## Explanation

Popularized by retirement researcher Dr. Wade Pfau and economist Zvi Bodie, this framework rejects the idea that a volatile stock and bond portfolio can safely guarantee a basic lifestyle. Instead, it segments your retirement goals into two strict categories: **Essentials** (housing, food, healthcare, taxes) and **Discretionary** (travel, hobbies, luxury spending).

You fund 100% of your essential expenses using "secure, stable, and sustainable" assets that do not rely on market performance—such as Social Security, pensions, Treasury Inflation-Protected Securities (TIPS) ladders, or lifetime income annuities. Once this guaranteed "income floor" is built, any remaining assets (the "upside") are invested aggressively in equities to fund discretionary goals and legacy wishes.

## Detailed Example

- **The Goals:** A couple requires $75,000 per year for absolute essentials and wants an additional $20,000 for leisure. They have a $1,200,000 nest egg.

- **The Income Floor:** Combined Social Security provides $45,000. This leaves a **$30,000 essential income gap** ($75,000 – $45,000).

- **The Allocation:** Under safety-first, they take $500,000 of their savings to buy a joint-life immediate annuity or build a 20-year TIPS bond ladder that contractually guarantees exactly $30,000 per year.

- **The Upside:** Their core survival is now entirely decoupled from Wall Street. They take the remaining $700,000 and invest it heavily in low-cost equity index funds. If the stock market drops 40%, they simply skip their vacations that year; their mortgage, healthcare, and grocery bills remain entirely funded.

## Advantages & Disadvantages

- **Advantages:** Eliminates the emotional panic of market volatility because your baseline lifestyle is contractually guaranteed. It removes reliance on "safe withdrawal rate" probabilities.
- **Disadvantages:** Buying annuities or locking money into government bonds requires giving up significant liquidity. If you pass away early in retirement, the wealth left to heirs can be lower than if you kept a traditional invested portfolio.

# The IRS Life Expectancy (RMD-Based) Method

## Explanation

This strategy treats your entire portfolio framework similarly to how the IRS mandates Required Minimum Distributions (RMDs). Every year on January 1st, you look up your age on the IRS Uniform Lifetime Table (or Single Life Table) to find your remaining life expectancy "divisor." You divide your total portfolio value as of December 31st of the previous year by this divisor to determine your income for the year.

Because your life expectancy naturally drops as you age, the divisor gets smaller, meaning your withdrawal *percentage* automatically increases over time. To avoid sharp spikes or drops in annual income from a single day's market closing price, planners often use a **Modified RMD Method** that uses a rolling 3-year average of your portfolio's value instead.

## Detailed Example

- **Setup:** A retiree is 73 years old with a total portfolio value of $1,000,000 on December 31st.
- **Calculation:** According to IRS Table III, the distribution period (divisor) for age 73 is **26.5**.
    - **Year 1 Income:** $1,000,000 ÷ 26.5 = **$37,736** (an effective withdrawal rate of 3.77%).
- **Fast Forward:** Ten years later, the retiree is 83. The IRS divisor drops to **17.7**. Let's assume poor market returns and past withdrawals mean the portfolio value has fallen to $850,000.
    - **Year 10 Income:** $850,000 ÷ 17.7 = **$48,022** (an effective withdrawal rate of 5.65%).

## Advantages & Disadvantages

- **Advantages:** It is mathematically impossible to run out of money because you are only ever withdrawing a percentage of what remains. It requires no complex software or high-fee products, and it naturally maximizes spending late in life when your horizon narrows.
- **Disadvantages:** Your annual income fluctuates in tandem with market performance, which can make fixed monthly budgeting difficult without an extra cash buffer. Additionally, if you retire before age 73, you have to manually map out custom life expectancy tables since formal IRS tables are optimized for older ages.

# The Home Equity / Reverse Mortgage Buffer Strategy (HECM Buffer)

## Explanation

This method uses a Home Equity Conversion Mortgage (HECM)—the federally insured version of a reverse mortgage—as a standby "buffer asset" to insulate an investment portfolio from market downturns.

Instead of borrowing a lump sum to spend immediately, you open a HECM **line of credit** at the start of retirement and leave it completely untouched. In years when the stock market is positive, you draw income from your portfolio normally. In years when the market enters a correction or a bear market, you stop portfolio withdrawals entirely and live off tax-free draws from your HECM line of credit. This gives your stock portfolio the necessary time to recover without being systematically forced to liquidate assets at depressed prices.

## Detailed Example

- **The Infrastructure:** A 65-year-old retiree has a $1,000,000 investment portfolio and a $500,000 home. They establish an approved HECM line of credit, which yields an initial available credit limit of roughly $220,000.
- **The Crisis:** In Year 3 of retirement, the stock market plummets 25%. Pulling their standard $45,000 annual living expense out of the portfolio during this downturn would lock in permanent losses and rapidly accelerate portfolio depletion.
- **The Buffer Strategy:** The retiree pauses portfolio withdrawals. They draw **$45,000 tax-free** from the HECM line of credit to cover expenses. The stock portfolio is left completely alone.

- **The Recovery:** Two years later, the market rebounds completely. The retiree resumes pulling income from the portfolio. They can choose to leave the HECM loan balance to be paid later from the eventual sale of the home, or they can use excess market gains during a subsequent bull market to pay down the line of credit and restore their buffer.

## Advantages & Disadvantages

- **Advantages:** Provides a powerful defense against sequence of returns risk. A major feature of the HECM line of credit is that the unused portion is guaranteed to grow over time at the current interest rate, independent of local housing market fluctuations. Furthermore, mortgage draws are non-taxable, keeping your Adjusted Gross Income (AGI) low.
- **Disadvantages:** Upfront closing costs (including FHA mortgage insurance premiums and origination fees) can be quite expensive. Compounding interest accrues on any borrowed balances, which ultimately reduces the final home equity left behind for heirs or future long-term care needs.

# Monte Carlo Simulation and Detailed Financial Planning Software

Traditional, free retirement calculators can use a dangerous shortcut: they assume your portfolio grows at a perfectly flat, linear rate (like 6% or 7% every single year). But the real world doesn't work that way. Markets move in jagged waves, and taxes chew through traditional IRAs far differently than they do Roth accounts.

This is where **detailed financial planning software** and **Monte Carlo simulations** come in. Instead of giving you a single, static guess, they stress-test your financial life against thousands of historical possibilities to see if your strategy holds water.

## How It Works: The Multi-Scenario Stress Test

A **Monte Carlo simulation** is a mathematical algorithm that injects randomness into your retirement timeline.

Instead of multiplying your current balance by a fixed rate of return, the software runs your exact portfolio blend through **1,000 or more simulated lifetimes**. Each simulation uses actual historical data to randomize the *sequence* of your returns.

- One simulation might mimic the roaring 1990s at the start of your retirement.
- Another might force you to retire right into a repeat of the 2008 financial crisis or the 1970s stagflation.

The software tracks how many of those 1,000 lifetimes your money successfully lasts to your target age (e.g., age 95 or 100). If your money survives in 900 out of those 1,000 randomized paths, the software assigns your plan a **90% Probability of Success**.

## Beyond the Simulation: What Advanced Software Layers In

Modern financial planning platforms do much more than simulate market returns. They function as a unified engine to model complex, intersecting real-world variables:

- **Tax-Aware Withdrawal Sequencing:** It maps out exactly *which* accounts to pull from first—taxable brokerage accounts, traditional tax-deferred IRAs, or tax-free Roths—to minimize your lifetime tax bill and avoid stealth costs like Medicare premium surcharges (IRMAA).
- **Social Security Optimization:** It analyses the exact "breakeven" age and portfolio impact of claiming benefits early at 62 versus waiting for a permanent 8% annual payout bump up to age 70.
- **Lumpy Expense Modelling:** It allows you to schedule distinct life events, such as higher travel expenses during your initial "Go-Go" retirement years, a vehicle purchase every 8 years, or downsizing a primary residence at age 75.

# Advantages of This Approach

- **Exposes Sequence of Returns Risk:** This is the tool's greatest strength. It reveals the devastating impact of hitting a bear market during your first few years of retirement—a reality that fixed-rate calculators completely hide.
- **Highly Flexible "What-If" Projections:** It allows you to adjust single variables on the fly to see their instant impact on your plan. You can instantly answer questions like: "*What if I delay retirement by 18 months?*" or "*What if inflation averages 4% instead of 2.5%?*"
- **Replaces Guesswork with Probability:** It shifts your mindset from a fragile guarantee ("I will have exactly $1.4 million at age 80") to a resilient probability ("There is an 88% chance my current spending plan survives worst-case economic climates").

# Disadvantages and Hidden Trapdoors

- **The "Garbage In, Garbage Out" Rule:** The output is only as reliable as your inputs. If you underestimate your baseline healthcare costs, provide an unrealistic life expectancy, or input inaccurate tax data, the software will confidently spit out a high success score that is structurally flawed.
- **Historical Data Bias:** Monte Carlo models rely entirely on the historical standard deviations and asset class correlations of the past 100 years. If the future global economy experiences an unprecedented structural shift, the historical models may understate your true risk.
- **Psychological Misinterpretation of "Failure":** A 15% "probability of failure" does not mean you have a 15% chance of waking up bankrupt and homeless at age 85. In reality, it means that in 150 out of 1,000 market paths, you would simply have to make early, tactical spending modifications (like applying the Guardrail Method) to keep the principal intact.
- **Over-Conservatism (The Leftover Wealth Trap):** Because these models are built to ensure you survive the absolute worst-case historical scenarios, planning for a 95%+ success rate often means you will finish retirement with millions of dollars left over—meaning you may have needlessly over-saved and spent extra years working.

**The Takeaway:** Detailed financial planning software shouldn't be treated as a crystal ball that predicts the future. Instead, treat it as a navigation system. You run the analysis before you retire to establish your baseline route, and then rerun it every year or two to adjust your speed and course based on real-world conditions.

# Summary

As you can see, there are many different ways to determine whether or not you are on track for retirement. The good news is that major financial institutions—such as Fidelity, T. Rowe Price, Vanguard, and Charles Schwab—all offer robust financial models and calculators to assist you.

I am not recommending any specific rule, approach, model, or company. Rather, I am urging you to do the research and put in the work. It is your retirement, and nobody is ever going to care about it as much as you do.

Keep in mind that your retirement journey is entirely unique, as are your lifestyle, spending habits, debt, risk tolerance, and health. Because of this, you must be incredibly thoughtful when planning your future and calculating exactly how much you need to save.

## My own Hybrid Approach

When I learned about all of these different approaches, I took a Hybrid approach to my retirement planning. Here are the steps I have taken:

- I started with a deep and detailed assessment of all of our expenses. I am a bit of a financial pack rat, so I had all the records and information to let me know where our baseline expenses stood and where the money was going. This allowed me to cut or reduce a number of unwanted expenses.
- Planned for large fixed and variable expenses (property tax, large home repairs, propane, future transportation and travel)
- I then did a gap analysis to incorporate future Social Security payments and account for other income streams.
- I worked with a financial planner to run Monte Carlo Scenarios and also took advantage of their detailed planning software.
- I applied the Bucket/Guardrail Strategy (with a Capital Preservation component).

# Retiree Regrets

Welcome to the crux of this book. The following sections contain the collective wisdom and real-world regrets of everyday retirees. To make this wealth of information easy to digest, I have organized it into eleven core categories.

The goal is simple: learn from their missteps so you can avoid the costly pitfalls that caused them pain, while identifying what they did right so you can replicate their success.

Within these chapters, you will find more than one hundred specific regrets. I encourage you to read every single one of them and carefully consider how their lessons will reshape your own retirement journey.

## Here are the eleven categories:

1. **The Identity & Career Exit Crisis**
2. **The Portfolio & Capital Preservation Blunders**
3. **The Tax, RMD, & "Cliff" Landmines**
4. **The Time Management & Daily Purpose Void**
5. **The Family Dynamics & Boundary Traps**
6. **The Spousal Friction & Cohabitation Adjustments**
7. **The Physical Vitality & Mobility Neglect**
8. **The Healthcare & Medical Blind spots**
9. **The Travel, Leisure, & Lifestyle Miscalculations**
10. **The Housing, Location, & Relocation Mistakes**
11. **The Social Circle & Community Isolation**

# 1. The Identity & Career Exit Crisis

**Summary:** Stopping a decades-long career cold turkey without a mental transition plan frequently triggers an existential shockwave. Retiring out of sudden frustration rather than a deliberate strategy causes individuals to collide with an immediate loss of prestige, structure, and cognitive stimulation, proving that walking away *from* a title is far harder than walking *toward* a purpose.

## Retiree Regrets

- Anchoring all of personal self-worth to a job, role or professional corporate title, leading to an immediate identity crisis on day one of retirement.
- Declining leadership or advisory positions on local civic or charitable boards out of temporary, post-work burnout.
- Ignoring the subtle mental stimulation that a career provided, leading to unexpected cognitive boredom or brain fog.
- Refusing to consult a professional therapist or counselor to navigate the profound sense of grief that can accompany leaving a long career.
- Constantly steering conversations back to old professional achievements to people who have no context or interest in them.
- Rejecting low-stress, part-time consulting or passion projects purely because you felt it was a step backward from a former title.
- Retiring abruptly based on a single bad day at the office, rather than working through a structured exit plan.
- Not retiring sooner
- Forgetting that a company will replace you in a week, but your family and friends never can
- Letting fear guide career decisions
- Not building professional network: missing opportunities and support later in life.

- Working too many hours: Realizing late that the extra pay wasn't worth the lost time.
- Prioritizing career and promotions over relationships and family
- Not spending enough time with family: Letting work or distractions crowd out everyday moments with loved ones.
- Choosing work over key family events: Missing graduations, performances, or milestones.
- Being consumed with work and projects in pursuit of promotions and respect at work, instead of being consumed with my family and relationships.

# 2. The Portfolio & Capital Preservation Blunders

**Summary:** Letting short-term market panic, trendy assets, or simple inertia override mathematical realities is a recipe for early retirement failure. Whether it is filing for benefits early out of anxiety, keeping money locked in zero-yield checking accounts, or refusing to transition from an aggressive growth strategy to an inflation-protected preservation framework, these missteps permanently erode purchasing power over a multi-decade horizon.

## Retiree Regrets

- Not starting retirement savings sooner
- Not saving a larger percent of income each pay check.
- Failing to calculate the compounding impact of an inflation rate on fixed income cash flows over a long-term timeline.
- Taking Social Security at the earliest age out of anxiety, rather than mapping the long-term break-even math of waiting for a larger guaranteed payout.
- Liquidating equities or mutual funds during a temporary market downturn out of panic, permanently locking in paper losses.
- Keeping an identical high-growth, high-volatility investment strategy past retirement day instead of shifting to an income-and-preservation framework.
- Concentrating too much retirement capital into a single asset class, such as an unhedged piece of real estate or a former employer's stock.
- Blindly trusting high-commission financial salesmen pitching complex, opaque annuity products with severe surrender charges.
- Failing to maintain a highly liquid cash or money-market buffer to navigate sequence-of-returns risk early on.

- Keeping too much money sitting in zero-yield checking accounts, letting purchasing power steadily erode against inflation. Not moving the cash to a higher interest Money Market account.
- Forgetting to audit life, home, and auto insurance policies annually, overpaying for coverage out of simple inertia.
- Making major financial choices based entirely on short-term news cycles rather than a comprehensive, decades-long horizon.
- Chasing Yield!
- Chasing the latest craze (e.g. crypto or AI)
- Not remembering that cash flow and capital preservation are key to retirement survival.
- Not moving quickly enough from a savings mentality to a spending mentality and setting up the pay check that you pay yourself.
- Not taking full advantage of employer matching funds and retirement planning resources.
- Failing to learn basic personal finance, budgeting, and long-term investment strategies when young.
- Not seeking financial advice from CPA or CFP
- Seeking and getting bad advice from family, friends and co-workers
- Overspending on lifestyle inflation
- Living beyond their means: Spending to impress others instead of building security.
- Taking on too much debt: Carrying credit card or loan balances that limited choices later.
- Cosigning loans unwisely
- Poor debt management
- Not having an emergency fund: Being one crisis away from serious hardship.
- Not planning for Sequence of Returns Risk No strategy for market downturns early in retirement
- Failing to have a plan for retirement
- Not including spouse/partner in retirement planning
- Not preparing for inflation and rising costs: Assuming today's expenses would stay the same.

- Not taking full advantage of Roth or HSA accounts
- Making emotional investment decisions
- Delaying Roth conversions or tax planning
- Poor investment choices Bad asset allocation, poor Roth conversions,
- Not investing consistently: Letting fear or confusion keep money in cash for decades.
- Cashing out retirement accounts prematurely: Paying penalties and losing future growth.
- Not talking about money with a partner: Leading to conflict, secrets, or misaligned expectations.
- Not balancing saving with living: Either over-saving and missing joys, or overspending and feeling unsafe.
- Not spending money to help save time and convenience.

# 3. The Tax, RMD, & "Cliff" Landmines

**Summary:** Treating taxes as a reactive annual task rather than a decades-long strategy leads to devastating financial penalties. Retirees often blindsidedly spike their lifetime tax rates and trigger massive Medicare surcharges by mishandling required minimum distributions, executing messy lump-sum account withdrawals, or ignoring the structural advantages of deliberate asset location.

## Retiree Regrets

- Misunderstanding how Required Minimum Distributions (RMDs) can unexpectedly push a household into a much higher income tax bracket.
- Triggering massive Medicare premium surcharges (IRMAA) by failing to space out large traditional tax-deferred account withdrawals.
- Not understanding Medicare two year look back at income to determine our premiums.
- Neglecting to establish a clear monthly tax-withholding strategy on retirement distributions, resulting in an expensive surprise in April.
- Paying off a low-interest mortgage early by taking a massive lump-sum retirement withdrawal that artificially spikes that year's tax bracket.
- Postponing estate planning conversations with a spouse and beneficiaries, leaving an administrative mess for survivors.
- Managing investments with zero regard for asset location, placing high-tax assets in standard taxable accounts.
- Not taking advantage of QCD for charity after turning 70 ½ to also help with RMDs.
- Not understanding the income brackets and cliffs for ACA medical marketplace coverage
- Not taking advantage of HSA and IRA to help lower MAGI to help avoid cliffs
- Not working with a professional CPA.

# 4. The Time Management & Daily Purpose

**Summary:** The ultimate dream of absolute freedom can quickly decay into an aimless, drift-heavy trap. Without a core creative anchor or an intentional daily structure, open schedules are easily swallowed by passive television consumption, obsessive news tracking, or everyday minor chores that expand to fill the void, turning an endless vacation into a source of cognitive boredom.

## Retiree Regrets

- Failing to construct a structured daily routine, causing retirement to feel aimless, repetitive, or drift-heavy.
- Falling into a passive habit of consuming round-the-clock television or political news feeds as a substitute for real-world engagement. Or worse, feeding on continuous financial news!
- Failing to find at least one deep, multi-hour "creative anchor" to replace work output.
- Letting everyday minor household chores expand into highly stressful, day-long projects just because there is no deadline.
- Forgetting how to sit comfortably in quiet reflection, constantly feeling an artificial urge to be hyper-productive.
- Letting cynicism regarding modern societal or cultural shifts replace a natural sense of curiosity and learning.
- Assuming deep personal fulfilment would just happen automatically without active experimentation and daily effort.
- Neglecting to practice conscious gratitude for the simple, unhurried elements of financial and time freedom.
- Saying yes to too many civic or charitable requests in the early part of retirement.
- Abandoning a complex new skill or hobby the moment you hit the initial learning curve.
- Viewing retirement as an endless, permanent vacation rather than an intentional, distinct second chapter of adult development.

# 5. The Family Dynamics & Boundary Traps

**Summary:** Out of misplaced guilt or a lack of personal boundaries, retirees frequently risk their own financial and calendar independence to subsidize the lifestyles of extended family. Co-signing major personal loans, acting as uncompensated, full-time childcare, or expecting independent adult children to pivot their lives around an open retirement schedule inevitably breeds deep resentment and financial vulnerability.

## Retiree Regrets

- Co-signing large personal loans or financing high-end cars for adult children using core retirement nest-egg cash.
- Lending money to extended family members under loose verbal agreements that ultimately sour the relationship.
- Overcommitting to full-time, uncompensated childcare for extended family out of guilt, completely surrendering personal retirement freedom.
- Expecting adult children to anchor their schedules around your open retirement availability.
- Letting old arguments or fights fester and becoming bitter
- Suppressing affectionate feelings and not saying "I love you" enough to family members.
- Assuming friends and family members already knew how much you appreciated them without saying it.
- Failing to offer a sincere apology to someone when you knew you were in the wrong.
- Failing to stand up for a partner or family member during a critical moment of need.
- Not telling people how much they meant to you while they were still healthy enough to hear it.
- Not saying “I love you” more often: Assuming people “just knew” instead of speaking it plainly.

- Not apologizing when they were wrong: Pride getting in the way of repairing relationships.
- Not speaking up in crucial moments: Staying silent during important family decisions or crises.
- Avoiding hard conversations about end-of-life wishes: Leaving loved ones uncertain and stressed.
- Constantly trying to "fix" or change a partner instead of accepting them as they were.
- Abandoning a relationship too quickly when things got difficult, rather than working through it.
- Forgetting to celebrate small victories, anniversaries, and joyful moments with loved ones.
- Taking loved ones for granted
- Not being present with grandchildren
- Not reconciling with estranged relatives and allowing family conflicts to continue
- Carrying unspoken guilt or secrets that created an invisible wall between you and your family.
- Not writing down or keeping physical records of meaningful family stories and memories.
- Drifting away from siblings: Losing touch over small disagreements or simple neglect.
- Not teaching children practical life skills and emotional resilience while they were under your roof.
- Failing to keep promises made to children or partners.
- Being too strict or harsh with children instead of leading with patience.
- Not supporting a child's unique dreams because they didn't match your own expectations.

# 6. The Spousal Friction & Cohabitation Adjustments

**Summary:** The sudden transition to 24/7 cohabitation can create an intense claustrophobia within even the strongest relationships. Assuming that free time will automatically heal historic friction—without actively communicating daily boundaries, carving out independent physical spaces, or maintaining separate social lives—turns mutual retirement into a high-friction roommate crisis

## Retiree Regrets

- Assuming a partner wants constant cohabitation without establishing clear independent hobbies, friendships, and personal physical spaces.
- Believing that an abundance of free time would automatically fix long-standing communication issues within a marriage or partnership.
- Failing to explicitly communicate personal daily boundaries, schedules, and alone-time preferences with a live-in partner.
- Relying entirely on a spouse or partner to organize all social engagements, trips, and weekend itineraries.
- Not spending enough one-on-one, undistracted quality time with a spouse in the years before retirement
- Not having quality discussions about how time would be allocated in retirement
- Taking a partner's daily efforts, care, and presence for granted over the years.
- Not making an effort to deeply understand a partner's interior world and personal passions.
- Not being emotionally open with a partner: Keeping feelings bottled up and creating distance.
- Hiding your true thoughts, struggles, or vulnerabilities from your partner to "keep the peace."
- Not dreaming and designing life together with spouse
- Not Starting retirement planning together as retirement neared

- Not having the courage to walk away from emotionally manipulative relationships earlier.
- Staying in an unhappy or toxic marriage for decades just out of fear of being alone or the fear of change
- Not showing appreciation to a spouse or partner: Taking everyday support for granted.
- Not expressing affection enough
- Choosing to be "right" in an argument rather than choosing kindness and connection
- Letting conflicts linger: Holding grudges instead of resolving arguments while there was still time.
- Losing your temper too quickly with loved ones over minor, insignificant household issues.

# 7. The Physical Vitality & Mobility Neglect

.

**Summary:** Assuming that physical health, balance, and joint mobility will automatically remain stable without focused daily effort is a dangerous retirement delusion. Neglecting regular resistance training, ignoring subtle changes in gate or posture, and letting poor nutritional habits slide directly compromises independent mobility—the literal baseline currency required to enjoy retirement freedom.

## Retiree Regrets

- Refusing to spend money on high-value convenience services (like heavy home maintenance or transport) as physical limits change out of stubborn habit.
- Completely letting go of regular sleep and wake schedules, which inadvertently triggers chronic sleep issues and low daytime energy.
- Letting minor shifts in seasonal weather keep you entirely indoors, becoming highly sedentary.
- Not learning how to cook simple, highly nutritious, enjoyable meals from scratch with your newfound free time.
- Falsely assuming your baseline physical health, balance, and energy levels will remain stable without focused daily effort.
- Stopping all forms of regular resistance or weight-bearing exercise, resulting in rapid muscle loss and fragile joints.
- Ignoring minor, persistent joint pain or slight gait changes instead of partnering with a physical therapist to address them early.
- Neglecting balance-specific training and core stability work, significantly increasing the long-term risk of a serious fall.
- Turning to increased, regular alcohol consumption as a primary coping mechanism for daily boredom or mild transition depression.
- Failing to consciously drink enough water throughout the day, ignoring that the body's natural thirst signals weaken naturally with age.
- Disregarding proper posture and ergonomic support while reading or watching screens at home, creating chronic back and neck issues.

- Wearing unsupportive, worn-out footwear during regular walks or around the house, slowly throwing off knee and hip alignment.
- Eating highly processed foods or ordering restaurant takeout constantly just because you have the time, consuming hidden sodium.
- Postponing basic home safety modifications until after an injury occurs.
- Believing you can easily "out-exercise" a highly inflammatory, poor nutritional diet.
- Carrying deep, constant mental anxiety about the natural aging process itself instead of focus-channelling energy into daily variables you control.
- Pushing through intense physical exhaustion during heavy landscaping or home lifting projects, causing completely preventable muscle tears.
- Allowing basic skin health to slide by neglecting to wear proper sun protection during hours of outdoor golf, gardening, or walking.
- Failing to build a professional physical therapy or sports-medicine partnership to fully rehabilitate minor strains before they permanently alter your movement.
- Forgetting that independent physical mobility is the absolute baseline currency required to spend your time and wealth exactly how you want.

# 8. The Healthcare & Medical Blind Spots

**Summary:** Managing wellness reactively or delaying minor medical adjustments out of pure vanity creates massive, irreversible health and financial liabilities. Failing to build financial bridges for early healthcare coverage, ignoring subtle cognitive or sensory declines like hearing and vision loss, and operating without legalized medical proxies leaves retirees wide open to preventable physical withdrawal and estate-draining crises.

## Retiree Regrets

- Not building a dedicated bridge fund to cover high health insurance premiums between early retirement and Medicare eligibility.
- Failing to formalize a clear, legal Power of Attorney and healthcare proxy before cognitive or physical changes occur.
- Skipping routine dental check-ups and cleanings, allowing minor issues to balloon into painful, highly expensive systemic complications.
- Delaying getting high-quality hearing aids due to personal vanity, which rapidly accelerates conversational withdrawal and cognitive decline.
- Staying with a general primary care physician who dismisses valid age-related lifestyle concerns instead of finding a geriatric specialist.
- Skipping regular comprehensive eye exams, missing subtle vision changes that can directly compromise night driving safety.
- Leaving chronic sleep conditions or snoring unaddressed, which permanently drains daytime cognitive focus and immune health.
- Skipping routine, age-appropriate preventative screenings out of simple avoidance anxiety.
- Failing to maintain a clear, updated, centralized master document of your medical history, surgeries, and active prescriptions for emergency personnel.

- Ignoring noticeable shifts in short-term memory or cognitive processing speeds instead of speaking openly with a neurologist early.
- Skipping standard seasonal vaccines or basic health protections right before boarding long, crowded international flights.
- Not taking full advantage of HSA accounts to save for medical expenses
- Neglecting mental health or refusing to seek professional therapy when struggling.
- Not taking care of their body earlier: Ignoring exercise, sleep, and nutrition until problems appeared.
- Not managing stress in healthier ways: Turning to work, food, or alcohol instead of coping skills.
- Not planning for caregiving needs: Being unprepared when they or a partner needed daily help.
- Not taking health warnings seriously: Ignoring early signs of heart, metabolic, or cognitive issues.
- Not staying active Physical and mental inactivity after retirement
- Taking good health for granted

# 9. The Travel, Leisure, & Lifestyle Miscalculations

**Summary:** Spending high-value early retirement years over-scheduling commitments, chasing peer-driven travel trends, or locking up liquid cash in massive, depreciating luxury toys frequently backfires. True fulfilment comes from pacing experiences to match physical energy, favoring off-season flexibility, and overcoming hyper-frugal anxieties to fund authentic, meaningful memories before physical limits set in.

## Retiree Regrets

- Sinking significant liquid cash into large luxury depreciating assets (like high-end boats or oversized motorhomes) that rarely get used.
- Assuming baseline retirement expenses will automatically drop, ignoring that early retirement travel often matches or exceeds pre-retirement spending.
- Delaying highly physical, long-distance "bucket list" travel trips until your late 70s, when joint mobility and endurance naturally decline.
- Over-scheduling the retirement calendar with back-to-back commitments, accidentally recreating the exact stress and fatigue of full-time work.
- Investing thousands of dollars into premium, top-tier equipment for a brand-new hobby before verifying you actually enjoy the daily practice of it.
- Booking rigid, high-stress group tours that offer zero personal flexibility, pacing choice, or spontaneous exploration.
- Traveling exclusively during high-peak travel seasons instead of using retirement flexibility to enjoy cheaper, quiet shoulder seasons.
- Traveling to specific destinations based entirely on peer trends rather than authentic, deep-seated personal interest.
- Letting a hyper-frugal mindset prevent you from spending money on rare, meaningful family experiences that you can easily afford.
- Failing to explore the parks, historical landmarks, and cultural venues located right in your own immediate home state.

- Accumulating more physical, material consumer goods rather than intentionally investing in memories and relational experiences.
- Postponing long-held creative plans because you falsely assume you have an infinite runway of perfect health.
- Traveling continuously without taking dedicated rest periods at home, leading to intense travel exhaustion.
- Failing to keep simple physical journals, photo albums, or personal records of your retirement adventures.
- Not traveling or going on family vacations while everyone was young and healthy.
- Saying "no" to spontaneous, exciting adventures because they felt slightly inconvenient.
- Not visiting specific dream destinations: Carrying a lifelong "someday" that never came.
- Not saying yes to small adventures: Turning down road trips, hikes, or spontaneous outings.
- Not trying new foods or cultures: Staying in their comfort zone instead of exploring.
- Not attending concerts, plays, or events they cared about: Missing "once in a lifetime" experiences.
- Not celebrating milestones properly: Letting birthdays, anniversaries, or achievements pass quietly.
- Not taking solo trips: Never learning how capable and independent they could be.
- Not making a "bucket list" earlier: Waiting too long to name and pursue big experiences.
- Not having hobbies  and go through life only working; then retire with nothing to do
- Spending too much time watching television
- Spending too much time online
- Not volunteering more

# 10. The Housing, Location, & Relocation Mistakes

**Summary:** Executing permanent, high-friction real estate decisions based on temporary emotional impulses or idealized vacations is a massive structural trap. Relocating to a trendy destination without testing its full seasonal cycle, buying dual-maintenance secondary properties, or neglecting to audit local medical infrastructure leaves aging retirees isolated in homes that no longer fit their physical or logistical realities.

## Retiree Regrets

- Neglecting to budget explicitly for major home maintenance variables over a multi-decade span.
- Relocating immediately to be near adult children, only for those children to move across the country for a new job opportunity.
- Moving permanently to a trendy vacation town or foreign destination without renting a home there for a full four seasons first.
- Selling a highly functional, long-term family home immediately upon retirement before understanding your actual post-work lifestyle needs.
- Buying an expensive piece of secondary real estate or a vacation timeshare that introduces double maintenance costs and limits travel variety.
- Letting major, multi-year home renovation projects consume the peak physical years of early retirement instead of prioritizing life experiences.
- Postponing down-sizing or decluttering an oversized house early, leaving a massive physical and emotional burden for your older self.
- Not dedicating a specific, separate room or zone in the home exclusively for independent hobbies, creating clutter in shared living spaces.
- Failing to carefully research the local specialized medical infrastructure of a remote town or country before relocating there.

# 11. The Social Circle & Community Isolation

**Summary:** Relying entirely on workplace relationships leaves a retiree deeply isolated the moment they exit the office door. Allowing old professional connections to go cold without actively investing the energy to build local community networks, conquer modern tech tools, or cultivate neighborhood peers causes an individual's daily world to rapidly shrink into deep loneliness.

## Retiree Regrets

- Allowing casual workplace friendships to go completely cold without replacing them with active, local community peers.
- Letting a fear of modern technology or social platforms isolate you from younger generations and digital community tools.
- Becoming a strict homebody and allowing subtle social anxieties to shrink your daily world.
- Allowing minor disagreements with neighbors or local groups to morph into long-term personal grudges out of boredom.
- Joining an excessive number of neighborhood or HOA boards purely out of habit, quickly draining your personal time.
- Hanging out with toxic or bitter people who only suck the life out of the room and bring you down.
- Not walking away from social commitments that felt more like an obligation vs. a real joy.
- Listening to advice from people who had no real experience or expertise.
- Not driving friends to appointments or cooking them a meal when they are ill.
- Not prioritizing relationships enough
- Letting friendships fade: Not making the effort to call, write, or visit.
- Neglecting to build a supportive, close-knit local community of nearby neighbors and friends.

# Golden Rules for Getting it Right

The purpose of this next section is to share everything retirees felt they got right—the choices they recommend you make and the positive habits they continue to practice in retirement. I call these the "Golden Rules." Just like the regrets, there are more than one hundred Golden Rules, beautifully organized into seven distinct subsections:

1. **Money & Practical Planning**
2. **Physical Health & Staying Strong**
3. **Family Dynamics & Loving Relationships**
4. **Friendships & Community Connections**
5. **Hobbies, Creativity & Continuous Learning**
6. **Travel, Leisure & Everyday Adventures**
7. **Giving Back, Mindset & Legacy Fulfillment**

In the previous chapter, you read about the heavy burdens of retiree regrets. Now, you have the opportunity to juxtapose those warnings with these Golden Rules. I hope this balance offers clear, actionable guidance as you map out your own retirement journey.

# 1. Money & Practical Planning

## Summary:

Transitioning from a regular pay check to a retirement portfolio can feel like a high-wire act, but it becomes incredibly manageable once you break it down into concrete steps. Here are practical ideas from retirees that can help you simplify your accounts, outsmart hidden fees, and build an impenetrable defensive shield around your hard-earned nest egg.

## The Golden Rules

- **Track your spending with a simple game plan:** Know exactly where your dollars go every single month instead of just guessing.
- **Wait a little longer to claim your retirement benefits:** Delaying your government checks for a few extra years makes each payment permanently bigger.
- **Gather all your old accounts into one place:** Merge scattered workplace accounts into a single dashboard so your money is easy to see and manage.
- **Wipe out high-interest debt before you call it quits:** Pay off credit cards and personal loans so your fixed income isn't eaten up by interest.
- **Try to pay off your house early:** Eliminating your mortgage payment instantly drops your monthly baseline living expenses.
- **Keep a solid "rainy day" cash stash:** Keep one to two years of living expenses liquid so you never have to sell investments during a market drop.
- **Watch out for high investing fees:** Move away from high-fee active managers and look for simple, low-cost options.
- **Know the rules about required withdrawals (RMD's):** Learn the government timelines for taking money out so you don't get hit with surprise tax penalties.
- **Set up a separate account just for healthcare costs:** Isolate cash specifically for medical needs to protect your everyday budget.

- **Grab extra insurance to cover what basic plans miss:** Secure supplemental coverage to cap how much cash you pay out of pocket for medical emergencies.
- **Set strict financial boundaries with your kids:** Learn to say "no" to adult children asking for loans that threaten your own core security.
- **Get your important legal paperwork in order:** Put your will, power of attorney, and medical directives in a safe, accessible spot.
- **Share the financial keys with your partner:** Ensure both spouses know passwords, account locations, and the overall game plan.
- **Fix up the house *before* you stop working:** Replace expensive items like roofs and water heaters while you still have a regular pay check.
- **Shop around for insurance every single year:** Compare home, auto, and health policies every autumn to stop companies from creeping your rates up.
- **Create a separate "fun money" bucket:** Keep your travel and hobby cash completely separate from grocery money to eliminate spending guilt.
- **Work with financial professionals:** If you are not comfortable planning your own retirement, then work with a CFP and CPA.
- **Start Saving NOW:** Make saving for retirement a top financial priority. If you started late, take advantage of the "catch up" provisions the government has provided.
- **Create your own pay check:** Use your retirement savings to create your own pay check and pay yourself on a regular basis.
- **Look for ways to save:** Take advantage of senior discounts (always ask) it is one of the perks of getting older.
- **Track all your subscription services:** You might be shocked how much you are spending each month on recurring fees. Eliminate duplication and unused/underused services
- **Comparison Shop:** The internet makes is very easy to save money by comparison shopping. Every dollar saved is a dollar that can be invested for retirement.
- **Give yourself permission to spend:** You have spent all your years saving for retirement, now give yourself permission to spend and enjoy the fruits of your labor.

## How to Get Started This Week

1. **Print out your last three bank statements.** Grab a yellow highlighter and mark every single recurring subscription or bill you don't actually use or need anymore. Cancel them today.
2. **Call your retirement benefit office or log online.** Get a clear printout of exactly what your monthly check will look like depending on the age you claim it.
3. **Create a "Password Binder."** Write down every financial website, username, password, and account number you own. Put this binder in a secure place and show your spouse or trusted family member exactly where it lives.

# 2. Physical Health & Staying Strong

## Summary:

Your physical health is the ultimate foundation of your retirement wealth; after all, an impressive nest egg doesn't mean much if you don't have the energy or mobility to enjoy it. Taking care of your body shouldn't feel like a grueling chore or a high-intensity boot camp—it is simply about building gentle, protective daily habits. To help you maintain your independence and maximize your vitality, I've pulled together the top health strategies shared by long-term retirees. These fifteen practical physical moves can help you keep your joints moving freely, protect your safety at home, and ensure you have the strength to fully participate in every adventure retirement throws your way.

### The Golden Rules

- **Walk every single day:** Keep your heart and joints healthy with low-impact, consistent daily neighborhood strolls.
- **Take up swimming or water exercise:** Build cardiovascular strength without putting harsh, heavy pressure on your knees and hips.
- **Use yard work and gardening to stay active:** Get outside, bend, stretch, and lift while growing plants to keep your muscles working naturally.
- **Work on your balance every week:** Practice simple balance exercises, Tai Chi, or gentle yoga to drastically lower your risk of falling.
- **Do light strength training to protect your bones:** Use simple resistance bands or light weights to keep your muscles strong enough for daily chores.
- **Never skip your regular doctor checkups:** Stay on top of annual screenings, blood work, and physicals to catch minor issues before they get big.
- **Get your eyes and ears tested regularly:** Keep your glasses and hearing aids updated so you stay fully connected to the conversations around you.

- **Take your medications exactly how they are prescribed:** Manage your prescriptions carefully, avoid skipping doses, and talk to your doctor about side effects.
- **Fix up your house to prevent tripping:** Secure loose rugs, upgrade to bright lighting, and add sturdy grab bars to your bathrooms.
- **Protect your sleep schedule like a hawk:** Aim for a rock-solid seven to eight hours of sleep nightly by keeping a calm, regular bedtime routine.
- **Drink plenty of water throughout the day:** Keep your kidneys healthy and avoid feeling dizzy by hydrating consistently, even if you don't feel thirsty.
- **Cook more meals at home using real foods:** Ditch the pre-packaged box meals and focus on simple cooking with whole ingredients.
- **Cut back on processed sugar and salt:** Protect your blood pressure and your daily energy levels by keeping sweets and sodium to a minimum.
- **Kick the smoking habit and tone down the alcohol:** Quit tobacco and moderate your drinking to give your liver, heart, and lungs a massive break.
- **Listen to your body and don't be ashamed to use helps:** Accept physical aids like braces, orthotics, or canes gracefully to keep yourself moving safely.

## How to Get Started This Week

1. **Walk through your house with a critical eye.** Pick up every single loose throw rug, clear clutter off the stairs, and replace any dim light bulbs with bright LEDs today.
2. **Buy a nice, sturdy 32-ounce water bottle.** Fill it up first thing in the morning and make it a game to finish it by lunchtime, then fill it again for the afternoon.
3. **Put a 10-minute walk on your daily schedule.** Pick a time—right after breakfast or right before dinner—and walk down your street and back. Rain or shine, get those steps in.

# 3. Family Dynamics & Loving Relationships

## Summary:

While securing your finances is critical, the true wealth of your retirement will ultimately be measured by the quality of your relationships. Leaving the working world gives you a beautiful opportunity to reconnect with the people who matter most, but navigating these changing family dynamics requires real intentionality. To help you cultivate deep, meaningful connections, I've collected the best relationship advice shared by experienced retirees. These fifteen intentional moves can help you strengthen your marriage, build unforgettable bonds with your grandkids, and create a warm, loving family anchor that lasts for generations.

## The Golden Rules

- **Put family time right on the calendar:** Stop leaving family connection to chance; set up fixed weekly calls or recurring dinner dates.
- **Move closer to the kids or grandkids if possible:** Relocate within an easy driving distance so you can be an everyday part of their lives.
- **Give your partner some breathing room:** Avoid smothering each other by ensuring both spouses have independent space and separate hobbies.
- **Keep having regular date nights:** Intentionally nurture your marriage with private trips, special dinners, and one-on-one time.
- **Take the grandkids for a weekend without their parents:** Give your adult kids a break while building deep, lasting bonds with the younger generation.
- **Host low-stress family get-togethers:** Ditch the high-pressure, formal holiday dinners and switch to casual potlucks and simple backyard barbecues.
- **Fix old family fights before it is too late:** Be the bigger person and reach out to estranged relatives to patch up old grudges.

- **Teach your grandkids old-school games and traditions:** Pass down classic board games, card tricks, and family recipes to bridge the generation gap.
- **Help your grown kids out, but don't pay for everything:** Provide an emotional safety net during a crisis without funding a lifestyle they haven't earned.
- **Have the tough talk about your future care wishes:** Sit down with your adult children to clearly explain your health, legal, and end-of-life choices.
- **Keep an "open-door" policy at your house:** Create a warm, friendly home where loved ones know they can drop by for a casual visit anytime.
- **Say "I love you" out loud and hug often:** Never assume your family just "knows" how you feel; tell them directly and show open affection.
- **Show up for the big milestones:** Make the effort to attend weddings, graduations, and major birthdays to show your people you care.
- **Be honest with your spouse about your fears:** Share your anxieties about aging, health changes, and life transitions instead of hiding them.
- **Practice letting go of tiny family annoyances:** Refuse to let small comments or minor family dramas ruin your time together with loved ones.

## How to Get Started This Week

1. **Call your adult children or a close relative tonight.** Don't wait for a holiday. Just call them up to see how their week is going and tell them you love them.
2. **Schedule a "just us" date night with your partner.** Plan a dinner or a scenic drive for this week, and agree that you are not allowed to talk about household chores, bills, or health issues during the date.
3. **Write down one family tradition you want to start.** It could be a monthly pizza night or a summer park day. Text the family group chat and get the first one on the books.

# 4. Friendships & Community Connections

## Summary:

Leaving the workforce solves the problem of a packed calendar, but it also removes a built-in community of colleagues. In retirement, maintaining a vibrant, active social life doesn't just happen by accident—it requires stepping out of your comfort zone and being intentional about who you surround yourself with. To help you stay connected, engaged, and supported, I've summarized the best social strategies from seasoned retirees. These fifteen practical moves can help you preserve your oldest friendships, foster new connections within your community, and build a protective inner circle that keeps life fun, active, and deeply fulfilling.

## The Golden Rules

- **Keep in touch with old friends from back in the day:** Prioritize regular phone calls, letters, and visits with the people who know your history.
- **Make new friends by joining local clubs:** Actively fight isolation by jumping into book clubs, hobby groups, or local senior center activities.
- **Get to know your immediate neighbors:** Build friendly, supportive relationships with the people on your block for mutual help and safety check-ins.
- **Learn how to use video calls to see distant loved ones:** Embrace basic modern technology so you can see the faces of family members who live far away.
- **Combine hanging out with healthy habits:** Form or join walking groups or exercise classes to get your social time and movement all at once.
- **Practice being a truly great listener:** Focus entirely on the other person when they speak, and skip the urge to give unprompted advice.

- **Walk away from toxic or dramatic friend groups:** Protect your peace of mind by steering clear of chronic complainers, gossips, and negative people.
- **Adopt a rescue pet for daily companionship:** Bring a dog or cat into your home for consistent structure, affection, and easy neighborhood socializing.
- **Meet up with old co-workers for lunch:** Keep a healthy, stress-free link to your old career by grabbing occasional coffees with former colleagues.
- **Join a local faith or spiritual group if that fits you:** Find a deep sense of belonging and value-driven support through a local place of worship.
- **Host small, casual hangouts at your place:** Keep life fun by organizing simple card nights, morning coffee chats, or casual dessert meetups.
- **Always show up for friends in times of grief:** Be there for your peers when they lose a spouse or go through hard times; your presence means everything.
- **Tell your friends face-to-face that you appreciate them:** Openly express your gratitude to your close buddies to strengthen your friendships.
- **Set healthy limits on your free time:** Guard your daily energy by politely declining to fill your calendar with endless favors and committees.
- **Drive friends to appointments or cook them a meal:** Step up and help your peers when they are sick or can no longer drive to build a powerful network of care.

## How to Get Started This Week

1. **Scroll through your phone contacts and find an old friend.** Send them a text or call them up out of the blue just to say, "Hey, I was thinking about you today. Let's catch up soon."
2. **Bake a quick batch of cookies or grab some fruit.** Walk over to a neighbor you haven't talked to in a while, knock on the door, introduce yourself, and have a five-minute chat.
3. **Look up one local group meeting this week.** Find a library book club, a senior center card game, or a church group. Put it on your calendar and commit to attending.

# 5. Hobbies, Creativity & Continuous Learning

## Summary:

Retirement gives you the ultimate luxury: complete ownership over your mental energy and creative focus. Keeping your mind active and engaged isn't just a great way to fill your days—it is a vital shield against cognitive decline and a proven way to find fulfillment outside of your old career. To help you lean into your curiosity, I've rounded up the best advice from retirees who have turned their post-work years into an era of personal reinvention. These fifteen practical moves can help you rediscover old talents, embrace the joy of being a complete beginner, and turn your days into an exciting classroom where your education never stops.

## The Golden Rules

- **Pick up a craft you used to love:** Spend time knitting, quilting, sewing, or crafting to keep your hands busy and create handmade gifts.
- **Try working with your hands:** Explore woodworking, furniture restoration, or model building to feel the deep satisfaction of creating physical objects.
- **Start painting, drawing, or working with clay:** Give yourself a creative outlet with simple, low-cost art supplies without worrying about perfection.
- **Don't be afraid to be a total beginner:** Give yourself permission to try completely unfamiliar activities and make mistakes with a smile.
- **Pick up a brand-new language:** Keep your brain firing by using free smartphone apps to learn a few foreign words every single morning.
- **Take a fun class at a local community college:** Take advantage of free or cheap senior tuition for interesting topics like creative writing or history.
- **Explore free online learning videos:** Use the internet to study scientific discoveries, master home repairs, or explore deep historical events for free.

- **Read books, newspapers, or magazines every single day:** Keep your mind sharp by reading a mix of fiction novels, biographies, and global news.
- **Pass down your specialized trade skills to younger folks:** Teach neighbors or youth the practical skills you mastered during your working years.
- **Set a massive personal challenge for yourself:** Give yourself a large goal to chase, like writing down your life story or finishing a giant project.
- **Enter your work into local county fairs or art shows:** Share your baked goods, garden veggies, or wood carvings at community events instead of hiding them.
- **Join a local book club or movie discussion group:** Force yourself to consume new types of media and debate big ideas with a friendly group.
- **Learn to play a musical instrument:** Pick up the guitar, piano, or ukulele; learning musical chords gives your brain an incredible workout.
- **Try out digital photography and photo editing:** Use your phone or a simple camera to capture nature, and learn how to organize pictures on a computer.
- **Learn the basics of the night sky:** Grab a pair of binoculars and a simple star map to identify constellations from your back porch.

## How to Get Started This Week

1. **Go to the public library.** Get a library card if you don't have one, walk over to a section you never visit (like ancient history or art), and pick out two books to take home.
2. **Download a free learning app on your phone.** Pick a language you always thought sounded cool, and complete the very first 5-minute lesson before you go to bed.
3. **Buy one basic hobby starter item.** Spend a few dollars on a sketchbook, a set of watercolor paints, or a simple puzzle. Set it on your kitchen table and spend 30 minutes playing with it.

# 6. Travel, Leisure & Everyday Adventures

## Summary:

For decades, your travel plans were strictly dictated by corporate holiday calendars, school breaks, and limited vacation days. In retirement, you finally hold the keys to complete geographic freedom. However, shifting from frantic, fast-paced vacations to meaningful, sustainable travel requires a completely different mindset. To help you navigate the open road smoothly, I've distilled the top travel secrets from veteran retirees who have mastered the art of exploration. These fourteen savvy moves can help you maximize your peak health years, outsmart peak-season pricing, and design unforgettable adventures that fit your energy levels and your budget perfectly.

## The Golden Rules

- **Do your biggest, most active trips early in retirement:** Don't delay your bucket-list vacations; travel while your physical energy and health are at their peak.
- **Mix grand vacations with simple day trips:** Keep life exciting without breaking the bank by taking day trips to nearby scenic towns and state parks.
- **Plan your travel around your favorite hobbies:** Center your vacations around your personal interests, like touring historic battlefields or visiting nature reserves.
- **Travel during the "off-season" to save big bucks:** Avoid school breaks to secure cheaper hotel rates, shorter lines, and peaceful, uncrowded destinations.
- **Take a special trip with just your grandkids or friends:** Create unique, lifelong memories by organizing a vacation without the parents around.
- **Keep a travel journal or make a photo album:** Write down the fun stories and preserve pictures from your journeys to look back on later in life.

- **Treat your own hometown like a tourist destination:** Spend your weekends exploring local museums, zoos, and cultural landmarks you normally ignore.
- **Go see America's beautiful National Parks:** Grab a lifetime senior pass to the National Parks for incredibly cheap, unlimited access to stunning public lands.
- **Try out a senior travel group where everything is planned:** Take the stress out of navigation and booking by joining a guided group tour for seniors.
- **Stay flexible and change your travel plans when you get tired:** Listen to your body and avoid packed itineraries; build regular rest afternoons into your trips.
- **Turn your travel into a fun reunion:** Plan your road trip routes around the towns where old friends and distant relatives live to reconnect over dinner.
- **Keep things simple by camping or renting a cabin:** Skip the expensive luxury hotels and reconnect with nature by renting a quiet cabin in the woods.
- **Sample new restaurants and types of food:** Keep life fresh by stepping outside your culinary comfort zone and trying brand-new types of food.
- **Document the unique history of the places you visit:** Read roadside historical markers and talk to locals to learn the true story of the towns you pass through.

## How to Get Started This Week

1. **Look up the lifetime Senior Pass for National Parks.** If you don't have one, find out how to order it online or buy it at a nearby park site. It is one of the best deals in America.
2. **Plan a "Hometown Tourist" day for this weekend.** Pick one museum, historic house, or beautiful garden in your city that you have never visited. Buy a ticket and go.
3. **Map out a simple day trip route.** Find a small town about 60 miles away that has an interesting diner or antique shop. Pick a clear day this week to drive out there for lunch.

# 7. Giving Back, Mindset & Legacy Fulfilment

## Summary:

Walking away from a full-time career leaves you with an incredible amount of freedom, but it also removes a major source of identity, routine, and daily purpose. Many retirees are surprised by how deeply they miss feeling needed, productive, and connected to something larger than themselves. True retirement satisfaction isn't about sitting idle—it is about redirecting your decades of wisdom, energy, and values into meaningful new channels. To help you navigate this emotional transition, I've pulled together the best advice from seniors who have successfully redefined themselves. These fifteen practical moves can help you build a healthy new routine, separate your self-worth from your old job title, and anchor your days in genuine joy and community purpose.

## The Golden Rules

- **Volunteer at a local school or library:** Spend a few hours a week tutoring kids or helping with book drives to keep your energy young and useful.
- **Help out at a local animal shelter:** Walk shelter dogs or care for cats to reduce your personal stress levels while helping animals in need.
- **Donate your time to a food bank or soup kitchen:** Give back directly to your community by sorting boxes or serving meals to neighbors going through hard times.
- **Use your old job skills to mentor younger workers:** Volunteer to help young adults practice interviews, build clean resumes, or learn basic business tools.
- **Join a local town committee or neighborhood board:** Put your lifetime of wisdom to good use by serving on town parks, library, or historic boards.
- **Take a fun part-time job that gives you energy:** Work a few hours a week at a golf course, hardware store, or boutique purely for the fun and social connection.

- **Start a small, low-stress passion business:** Turn a beloved hobby into a tiny side hustle, like selling fresh garden vegetables or custom wood carvings.
- **Separate your identity from your old job title:** Learn to value yourself for who you are as a human being, friend, and parent, not what you used to do for work.
- **Build a loose daily routine so you don't get lazy:** Establish a comfortable weekly rhythm with set times for chores, hobbies, and relaxation so days don't blur.
- **Practice saying "no" to commitments that drain you:** Guard your retirement freedom fiercely by politely declining favors or projects that feel like heavy burdens.
- **Actively look for small moments of joy every single day:** Train your mind to pause and appreciate micro-joys like a quiet morning, a warm sunset, or a good book.
- **Laugh at yourself and don't take aging too seriously:** Accept the grey hair, popping joints, and senior moments with a sense of humor instead of getting bitter.
- **Talk openly about your feelings of sadness or loneliness:** Reach out to a spouse, close friend, or therapist when the retirement transition feels heavy or lonely.
- **Focus on what you did right in life, not your old mistakes:** Refuse to let old regrets ruin your present peace; view your life story as a cohesive, wonderful success.
- **Write down your values and life lessons for your family:** Record your childhood memories, life lessons, and love for your descendants so they always have your guidance.

## How to Get Started This Week

1. **Call or visit one local charity or non-profit group.** Ask them what their biggest volunteer need is right now, and see if you can sign up for just one 2-hour shift next week.
2. **Buy a simple, blank notebook.** Sit down at your kitchen table with a cup of tea, and write down the full story of your very first job, your favorite childhood pet, or how you met your spouse.
3. **End your day with three specific "thank-you".** Right before you turn off the lights to go to sleep tonight, name three tiny things that happened today that you are genuinely grateful for.

# Retirement Vision

When people plan for retirement, they usually spend almost all of their time staring at spread sheets, calculators, and bank statements. But the math is only half the puzzle. If you don't figure out what you are actually saving *for*, you are building a financial bridge to nowhere.

Defining your "retirement vision" means painting a clear picture of your future life so you can put an accurate price tag on it. Here are the core questions every retiree should ask themselves, broken down into five simple categories.

## 1. The Clock: How will you fill your days?

When you retire, you instantly get an extra 40 or 50 hours of free time every single week. That sounds amazing, but a lack of structure can quickly lead to boredom.

- **What will get you out of bed on a rainy Tuesday morning?** Think about what you are retiring *to*, not just what job you are running *away* from.
- **What is on your "bucket list," and when do you want to do it?** Are you planning big, expensive international trips during your early "go-go" years, or do you prefer quiet, low-cost hobbies like gardening and reading?
- **Do you want to keep working in some way?** Many retirees choose to work part-time, consult, or start a small business just to stay mentally sharp and be part of a team.

## 2. The Map: Where is your home base?

Where you choose to live dictates your daily expenses, your taxes, and how you spend your time.

- **Do you want to "age in place" or downsize?** Will you stay in your current family home, or move to a smaller, single-story townhouse that requires less maintenance and yard work?
- **Are you moving for the right reasons?** If you are thinking about moving to a state with lower taxes, have you factored in the emotional cost? Will you end up spending all your tax savings on plane tickets to visit your kids and friends?

## 3. The Crew: Who are you sharing this life with?

Retirement completely changes your daily social life. Your inner circle will shift when you stop seeing co-workers every day.

- **Are you and your spouse on the same page?** If you are married, have you actually talked about your daily routines? One person might want to travel non-stop, while the other might just want to sit on the back porch. Mismatched expectations can cause major stress.
- **How will family impact your timeline?** Do you plan to spend significant time babysitting grandchildren? Is there a chance you will need to step in as a financial supporter or caregiver for an aging relative?

## 4. The Mirror: Who are you without your job?

For decades, your identity and self-worth were likely tied to your career. When people ask "What do you do?", you had an easy answer.

- **How will you replace the sense of purpose your career gave you?** If your job made you feel important or helpful, look for new ways to get that feeling. Can you volunteer for a cause you care about, mentor younger people, or take leadership roles in your local community?
- **What have you always been curious to learn?** Retirement is the perfect time to go back to school, learn an instrument, or master a new skill purely for the fun of it.

## 5. The Shield: What is your backup plan?

A great retirement vision needs to be flexible because life rarely goes exactly according to script.

- **What are you willing to cut if the stock market drops?** If your investments take a hit right after you retire, do you know which "discretionary" expenses (like big vacations or dining out) you can easily pause to protect your savings?
- **How will you protect your physical health?** Staying active and eating well isn't just about living longer—it is about preserving your ability to enjoy the travel and hobbies you planned. Have you factored the rising cost of healthcare into your lifestyle choices?

## 6. The End : What is your Legacy?

**What kind of financial legacy do I want to leave?** (Inheritances for children or family, charitable donations, or spending down assets?)

**The Takeaway:** The happiest retirees don't just plan their money; they design their days. Close your eyes and imagine your life ten years from now. Where are you? Who are you with? What are you doing? Once you can answer those questions, the financial planning part becomes much easier.

# Investment Policy Statement

What is an Investment Policy Statement (IPS)? It sounds fancy, doesn't it? In reality, it is simply a personalized roadmap that dictates exactly how you will manage and invest your money. It is all about having a written set of rules to keep you grounded, focused, and positioned for success.

Having a formal, written strategy is a massive competitive advantage. According to a study by the American College of Financial Services, only about 34% of savers actually have a written retirement income plan. By taking the time to draft an IPS, you immediately put yourself ahead of the curve.

## The Ultimate Promise to Yourself: The Investment Policy Statement (IPS)

Imagine walking into a grocery store when you are absolutely starving, without a shopping list. What happens? You fill your cart with chips, cookies, and frozen pizzas because they look amazing *right now*. You completely forget that your goal was to buy ingredients for a healthy dinner.

Investing for retirement can feel exactly like that. When the stock market is booming, everyone wants to buy into the latest hot trend. When the stock market crashes, panic sets in, and people want to sell everything and hide their cash under the mattress.

To keep from making huge mistakes driven by fear or excitement, you need a personal "shopping list" for your money. In the financial world, this is called an **Investment Policy Statement (IPS)**.

## What is an Investment Policy Statement?

An Investment Policy Statement is simply a written rulebook that outlines how you will manage your money. It does not have to be a long, boring document filled with fancy legal words. In fact, for most regular people, a single page is plenty.

Think of it as a contract you sign with yourself while you are calm, relaxed, and thinking clearly. It states exactly what your long-term goals are, how much risk you are willing to take, and exactly what types of investments you will use to get there.

## How Does It Work?

An IPS works by taking the guesswork out of daily financial decisions. Instead of waking up, watching a scary news report about the economy, and wondering, "*Should I sell my stocks today?*" you simply open your IPS.

Your IPS will already have the answer written down. For example, it might say: "*I will keep 40% of my money in safe short-term bonds and 60% in a diversified stock fund, no matter what the news says.*"

It sets the boundaries. If the stock market goes up and your stocks suddenly make up 75% of your total wealth, your IPS will tell you exactly when and how to "rebalance" — which means selling some stocks to buy more bonds to get back to your original, safe plan.

# Why You Absolutely Need One

- **It Stops Panic Decisions:** When the market drops, it is human nature to get scared. An IPS acts like an anchor in a storm. It reminds you of your long-term strategy so you don't sell low out of fear.

- **It Cuts Out the Noise:** Every day, TV hosts and internet influencers will tell you about the "next big thing." Your IPS is your shield. If a trendy new investment does not fit your written rules, you don't buy it. Period.

- **It Keeps Couples on the Same Page:** If you are married, writing an IPS together ensures you both agree on the financial game plan. One person won't accidentally risk the savings on a whim while the other thinks the money is sitting safely in a money market fund.

## Anatomy of a Personal Investment Policy Statement

| IPS Component | What It Defines | Example Target |
|---|---|---|
| **1. The Financial Goal** | The clear, underlying purpose of the money. | *"To fund a $75,000/year lifestyle in retirement without depleting principal."* |
| **2. Asset Allocation** | The specific mix of stocks, bonds, and cash. | *"Maintain a balanced portfolio of 60% equities and 40% fixed income."* |
| **3. Risk Tolerance** | Maximum acceptable drawdown before altering course. | *"Accept short-term market drops of up to 20% without panic-selling."* |
| **4. Rebalancing Trigger** | The rule for when to buy/sell to restore your mix. | *"Rebalance the portfolio every December, or if allocation drifts by more than 5%."* |

# A Practical Example of an IPS

Here is what a simple, real-world Investment Policy Statement looks like for someone focused on a safe, steady retirement.

**1. My Financial Goal**

My goal is to protect the money I have saved for retirement so it lasts the rest of my life. I want to generate steady income to cover my monthly expenses without stressing over daily market changes.

**2. Target Asset Mix (Where My Money Goes)**

To balance safety with a little bit of growth to beat inflation, I will stick to this target mix:

- **10% Cash / Money Market Accounts:** For easy-access emergency savings and daily living.
- **50% Short-Term Bonds:** For steady income and ultimate capital preservation (safety).
- **40% Low-Cost Stock Mutual Funds/ETFs:** To allow my money to grow slightly over time so I don't lose purchasing power.

**3. My Philosophy (The Rules I Live By) - Risk Tolerance**

- I do not try to time the market or guess where stocks are going next.
- I focus only on things I can control: keeping investment fees as low as possible and staying diversified.
- I prefer simple, safe investments like high-quality short-term bonds, money market funds, and broad stock market index funds.

**4. Rebalancing Plan**

Once a year, in December, I will look at my accounts. If market swings have caused my stock percentage to rise above 45% or drop below 35%, I will buy or sell just enough to get right back to my 40% stock target. I will not trade at any other time of the year based on market headlines.

# Who has an IPS?

In the world of finance, there is no official government headcount for how many retirees have a personal **Investment Policy Statement (IPS)**. Because an IPS is a personal document you write for yourself, nobody tracks them the way they track bank accounts or 401(k) plans.

However, major industry studies look at how financial advisors and everyday savers use them, and the numbers show that having a written rulebook is **rare** for everyday investors.

Here is what the actual data tells us:

## 1. Most Financial Advisors Don't Even Use Them

You might think that if you hired a professional, they would automatically give you an IPS. But a landmark industry study conducted by **Russell Investments** found that **61% of financial advisors in the United States do not create a written Investment Policy Statement for their clients**.

That means only about **39%** of people who actually pay for professional financial advice have a formal IPS in place. For every day, DIY (do-it-yourself) investors who manage their own money, the percentage is estimated to be dramatically lower.

## 2. General Written Plans Are Also Rare

An IPS is a specific kind of rulebook just for your investments. If we widen the lens to look at *any* kind of written retirement strategy (which includes things like budget planning and health care), the numbers are still surprisingly low.

According to a national survey by **The American College of Financial Services**, only **34% of everyday savers have a written retirement plan** of any kind. The other 66% are essentially "winging it" or keeping the plan entirely in their heads.

# A Final Thought on IPS

There is a saying from legendary coach John Wooden:

*"When you fail to prepare,*

*you're preparing to fail".*

If you don't take the time to map out your journey, how can you ever expect to arrive at your ideal retirement destination? Sit down and dedicate the time to draft your personal IPS. Combined with a clear retirement vision, this written framework will position you for long-term success—even in an unpredictable financial world.

# The Path Forward

Equipped with the hard-won feedback and collective wisdom of real retirees, the question now is: *How do you move forward?*

While every journey is unique, here is the foundational blueprint to get you started. Consider these your retirement basics:

- **Communicate with your partner:** Have an open conversation with your spouse or partner about your collective future, and commit to being equal partners throughout the planning process.
- **Define your vision:** Start by clarifying exactly what you want your day-to-day life to look like in retirement.
- **Know your risk tolerance:** be prepared to make adjustments as your age and as circumstances change.
- **Draft your Investment Policy Statement (IPS):** Use a written framework to define your financial goals, and consider partnering with a Certified Financial Planner (CFP) to sharpen it.
- **Assemble your advisory team:** Build long-term relationships with a trusted CFP, a CPA to help navigate tax strategies, and an estate attorney to secure your legal legacy.
- **Commit to continuous learning:** Never stop educating yourself on retirement strategy, as tax laws and financial regulations constantly evolve.

- **Pace yourself for a marathon:** Remind yourself daily that building a secure retirement is a long-term endurance race, not a short-term sprint.
- **Harness the power of time:** Let compounding do the heavy lifting by committing to consistent, dedicated investing from every single paycheck.
- **Aggressively eliminate debt:** Pay off liabilities as quickly as possible to maximize your monthly savings rate.
- **Capture your company match:** Never leave free money on the table; contribute enough to maximize any workplace retirement matching programs.
- **Protect yourself with an emergency fund:** Build a robust cash reserve, guard it fiercely for true emergencies, and replenish it immediately if you have to draw from it.
- **Nurture your key relationships:** Invest deeply in your bonds with family and friends long before you ever leave the workforce.
- **Guard your time:** Time is your most precious, unrenewable commodity. Be intentional with how you spend it today, and how you intend to deploy it tomorrow.
- **Discover your retirement purpose:** Identify your core passions and potential projects well in advance of your target date so you hit the ground running.

# Check List

Having explored both the deepest regrets of retirees and the Golden Rules they lived by, you are now ready to design—or refine—your own personal retirement roadmap.

The timeline below provides a clear, chronological framework of the critical actions you should take as you approach your target date. We will begin at the ten-year horizon, counting down step-by-step to your final day of full-time work, before mapping out the essential milestones to focus on during your actual distribution years and beyond.

If you are under fifty-five, time is entirely on your side to execute this strategy with precision. But even if you have already crossed fifty-five, you still have plenty of runway to make massive, meaningful adjustments and finish strong.

Think of this not as an exhaustive regulatory manual, but as a curated master plan of the high-impact, non-negotiable milestones that deserve your primary focus at each distinct stage of the journey. Since each retirement journey will be unique, you will need to fill in your own gaps.

Here are the timelines we will review:

- **10+ Years before retirement**
- **5-10 Years before retirement**
- **2-5 Years before retirement**
- **1-2 Years before retirement**
- **Last Year before retirement**
- **1-3 Months before retirement**
- **First Year before retirement**

# 10+ Years Before Retirement

- Discuss and align with your spouse or partner on all retirement plans. Ensure they know exactly where vital documents, financial files, usernames, passwords, and digital backup information are located.
- Consider automatic annual increases to your retirement savings. Many companies and platforms have the ability to automate this for you. These are the years to build your nest egg and take advantage of time and compounding.
- Increase Savings & Begin Catch-Up Contributions (Age 50+)
- Review Social Security Earnings Annually
- Review your different retirement accounts and determine best mix among tax-deferred, tax-free and taxable accounts based on the flexibility you desire.
- Maximize retirement savings and take advantage of any company matching
  - 401(k)
  - 403(b)
  - Traditional IRA
  - Roth IRA
  - HSA (if eligible)
- Review Asset Allocation
- Evaluate whether your investments match your retirement timeline and risk tolerance. As retirement approaches, sequence-of-return risk becomes more important.
- Consider developing a relationship with CFP and or CPA - even if it just to start the conversation and initial evaluation.
- Develop you Investment Policy Statement (IPS) and Retirement Vision

# 5–10 Years Before Retirement

- Discuss and align with your spouse or partner on all retirement plans. Ensure they know exactly where vital documents, financial files, usernames, passwords, and digital backup information are located.

- Clarify Retirement Lifestyle & Goals

- Review All Retirement Accounts

- Increase Savings Rate and begin to build cash buffer of 1-3 years' worth of cash for expenses.

- Estimate Retirement Spending - Create an annual retirement budget including:
    - Housing
    - Utilities
    - Streaming services
    - Phone/internet
    - Entertainment
    - Food
    - Transportation
    - Travel
    - Healthcare
    - Taxes
    - Gifts
    - Hobbies
    - Insurance

- Run Retirement Income Projections Estimate income from:
    - Social Security
    - Pension
    - Rental properties
    - Annuities
    - Investment withdrawals
    - Part-time work

- Develop an income plan rather than focusing only on account balances – how will you pay yourself in retirement?

- Create an income Withdrawal Strategy - decide:
    - Which accounts will be used first
    - Taxable account withdrawals
    - Traditional IRA/401(k) withdrawals
    - Roth withdrawals
    - Roth conversion opportunities

- Consider developing a relationship with CFP and or CPA - even if it just to start the conversation and initial evaluation. If you already have a relationship, consider how to get the maximum benefit to help you with your planning.

- Review ISP and Retirement Vision annually

- Review all insurance policies:
    - Home
    - Auto
    - Life
    - Umbrella
    - Other insurance products

- Start to decrease and or reduce credit card and personal loans and debt.
- Accelerate paying off home mortgage.

# 2-5 Years Before Retirement

- **Discuss and align with your spouse or partner on all retirement plans.** Ensure they know exactly where vital documents, financial files, usernames, passwords, and digital backup information **are** located.
- Estimate Retirement Income vs. Expenses and build realistic budget for retirement.
- Consider how you will Insulate Against "Sequence of Returns Risk": Review and rebalance your asset allocation. Gradually shift a portion of your wealth out of volatile equities and into more stable fixed-income holdings, short-term bonds, or money market instrument. This is where professional support can be most helpful, especially if you are not yet comfortable with financial acumen.
- Evaluate Healthcare Options Before Medicare -If retiring before 65 and don't have healthcare, then spend time to research ACA marketplace or COBRA.
- Create a My Social Security account and estimate Social Security benefits.
- Plan Social Security Claiming Strategy (which age to take distributions)
- Stress-Test Your Retirement Budget by living on your projected retirement income for several months.
- Major Home Repairs - Complete large projects while still employed:
    - Roof
    - HVAC
    - Water heater
    - Appliances
    - Vehicles

- Verify Beneficiaries and review:
  - 401(k)
  - IRA
  - Brokerage accounts
  - Life insurance
  - Bank accounts

- Continue Building a Cash Reserve
  - 1-3 years of spending needs
  - High-yield savings
  - Money market funds
  - Short-term Treasuries

- Review Estate Planning Documents and make any updates:
  - Will
  - Trust
  - Durable Power of Attorney
  - Healthcare Power of Attorney
  - Living Will

- Evaluate Housing Decisions - Determine whether you will:
  - Stay in current home
  - Downsize
  - Relocate
  - Move near family

- Review and refine ISP and Retirement Vision annually – make any necessary adjustments.

## Retirement Income Planning

• Around 5 years to retirement, create a list of your retirement income sources and a plan for managing healthcare costs.

• If you're approximately five years away from your anticipated retirement age, it's time to take a very close look at your finances, think carefully about the details of your retirement plan, and make some important decisions.

## Debt Reduction

• At the 5-year milestone before retirement, you may want to include maximizing contributions to your retirement plans or paying down unsecured debt, such as credit cards.

## Social Security Strategy

• Unlike other income sources, Social Security is income you cannot outlive. It also has the backing of the federal government and is protected against inflation. Deciding when to file for it is a critical step in retirement planning. Although you can start collecting benefits at age 62, you may want to consider delaying, depending on your circumstances.

## Healthcare Cost Planning

• Health care is a major expense in retirement. Use this time to review long-term care coverage or health-related spending accounts, and update healthcare plans.

## HSA Contributions

• A Health Savings Account (HSA) gives you triple tax benefits – tax-deductible contributions, tax-deferred growth, and tax-free withdrawals when you use the money to pay for qualified medical expenses. If you are eligible (you have to have a high-deductible health insurance plan), it can be an excellent place to stash your money.

## Lifestyle Vision

• When it comes to retirement planning, everyone's goal is pretty much the same: create a plan so that you may live happily and comfortably in your non-working days. You need to make it much more specific, set priorities, and visualize exactly the future you want – your beliefs, what you care about most, and how you want to spend your time in retirement and with whom.

# 1–2 Years before Retirement

- **Discuss and align with your spouse or partner on all retirement plans.** Ensure they know exactly where vital documents, financial files, usernames, passwords, and digital backup information **are** located.

- Medicare Enrollment Planning (Age 65)

- Pressure test your retirement plan again by living on your retirement budget for several months

- Decide Between Medicare Advantage vs. Original Medicare + Supplement and Review Part D (prescription drug coverage)

- Review Tax Planning Strategy and your Plan withdrawal order: e.g. *taxable → tax-deferred → tax-free.*

- Prepare for Required Minimum Distributions (RMDs)

- Finish Paying Off High-Interest Debt (credit cards, loans etc.)

- **Finalize Health Insurance Strategy** - If retiring before Medicare:

    - ACA Marketplace coverage
    - COBRA
    - Employer retiree health coverage
    - Spouse's employer plan

- **Finalize When to Claim Social Security** - Evaluate:

    - Age
    - Health
    - Spouse's benefits
    - Longevity expectations
    - Tax situation

- **Prepare a Retirement Pay check Plan** - Document:
    - Income sources
    - Monthly withdrawal plan
    - Tax withholding strategy
    - Emergency reserves

- Consider your purpose and how you will spend your time in retirement (volunteer work, hobbies, travel etc)

- Establish, build and or maintain personal relationships outside of work

- Review ISP and Retirement Vision annually - make any necessary adjustments

<u>Major Purchases</u>

• **Pre-fund major lifestyle and capital expenses.** Anticipate and aggressively address big-ticket items—such as roof replacements, major home renovations, appliance upgrades, or vehicle purchases—during your final one to three years in the workforce. Front-loading these major cash outlays during your peak earning years allows you to absorb the hit using active salary rather than investment capital. By clearing the deck of these predictable, heavy expenses before you step away from the paycheck, you prevent sudden cash-flow shocks exactly when your portfolio is at its most vulnerable.

<u>Asset Allocation Review</u>

• Once you're less than 2 years to retirement, set your retirement date, decide when you'll take Social Security, and review your asset allocation.

<u>Withdrawal Rate Strategy</u>

• Know where you will be pulling from (401k, IRA, Roth, and Brokerage Account etc.), what order you will pull out the money and exactly how much money you will need.

## Employer Stock & Pensions & Other Benefits

- Obtain documentation from your company related to stock options (and other long term incentives) so you understand important dates associated with each, such as vesting and expiration. Obtain all pension benefits available through your current employer.
- Work with your employer to better understand all the benefits you may receive in retirement.
    - Transition assistance
    - Retirement planning
    - Life insurance
    - Medical and Dental coverage

# Last Year Before Retirement

- **Discuss and align with your spouse or partner on all retirement plans.** Ensure they know exactly where vital documents, financial files, usernames, passwords, and digital backup information **are** located.

- Finalize Social Security Claiming Decision -Evaluate whether to claim at 62, FRA, or 70 (or some age in between)

- Review All Insurance Policies

    - Life insurance
    - Long-term care insurance
    - Homeowners/auto
    - Umbrella liability

- Complete Estate Planning Updates

- Organize Important Documents

    - Store in a secure location
    - Back up all computer files (physical and cloud)
    - Share instructions with executor or trusted person

- Schedule a Formal Consultation with Human Resources: Meet with your company's HR department to officially verify your benefit extensions.

- **Review Employer Benefits** - Determine what happens to:

    - Health insurance
    - Dental insurance
    - Vision insurance
    - Life insurance
    - HSA
    - Stock options and other long term incentives
    - Pension elections

- **Finalize Pension Decisions** - If applicable:
    - Lump sum
    - Single life pension
    - Joint survivor pension
    - These decisions are often irreversible.

- **Create final Retirement Budget**
    - Essential expenses
    - Discretionary expenses
    - Travel budget
    - Emergency reserve
    - Housing
    - Utilities
    - Streaming services
    - Phone/internet
    - Entertainment
    - Food
    - Transportation
    - Travel
    - Healthcare
    - Taxes
    - Gifts
    - Hobbies
    - Insurance

**Retirement Date & Income Gap Analysis**

• Examine guaranteed sources of income in retirement, such as Social Security and pension payments, as well as potential income from sources like retirement plans and investments. Compare total expected income against estimated expenses. . If there is a gap, work with a financial professional to explore options for closing the gap.

**Healthcare Bridge (If Retiring Before 65)**

• If you are retiring before age 65, make sure you can find affordable medical coverage to bridge you to Medicare eligibility.

## Medicare Enrollment (if you are turning 65)

• There are 3 enrollment periods for Medicare. It's important to sign up as soon as possible to avoid penalties or gaps in coverage. You enroll through Social Security.

## Estate Plan Review

• Your estate plan should reflect your current wishes. Review and update wills, beneficiaries, and related documents to ensure your wishes are honored and your loved ones are protected.

## Debt Elimination

• High-interest debt can quickly erode your retirement savings – aim to eliminate it before your income drops.

## 401(k) Rollover Planning

• Coordinate with your financial advisor on a plan for your 401(k) and other accounts held through an employer. If rolling funds to an outside IRA, open a new account and obtain account number and custodian address and wire instructions for future deposit. If retiring between 55 and 59½, you may want to wait to rollover due to options to take penalty-free withdrawals from a 401(k) in the year of retirement.

## Submit Paperwork

• State employees and many private-sector workers should begin the formal retirement process 12 months before their target retirement date. Many retirement systems recommend submitting paperwork 60 to 90 days before retiring.

# 1-3 Months Before Retirement

- **Final Employment Tasks** - Confirm:
  - Last paycheck
  - Vacation payout
  - Sick leave payout
  - Retirement account rollover options

- **Review Tax Plan** - Estimate:
  - Federal taxes
  - State taxes
  - Roth conversions
  - IRMAA exposure

# First Year of Retirement

- **Monitor Spending Monthly** - Compare:
  - Budgeted spending
  - Actual spending

- **Review Investment Allocation** - Confirm:
  - Cash reserves
  - Bond allocation
  - Equity allocation
  - Withdrawal rate

- **Review Annually** - Every year:
  - Social Security strategy
  - Medicare coverage
  - Investment allocation
  - Estate plan

- Beneficiaries
- Tax strategy
- IPS and Retirement Vision

**Required Minimum Distributions (RMDs)**

• Depending on your age (70 ½ - 75) and you own a tax-deferred retirement account, you must make minimum annual withdrawals. Make sure you've calculated what your required minimum distribution (RMD) should be this year and taken it in time. Failing to withdraw the full amount can result in hefty tax penalties.

**Charitable Giving from IRAs**

• If you're required to take a distribution but don't need the cash, you can give up to $108,000 from your IRA to a qualified charity in 2025 if you're at least age 70½. The amount isn't included in your taxable income, as an IRA distribution typically would be. This is called a QCD – Qualified Charitable Distribution (Donation).

**Annual Financial Review**

• Your retirement plan isn't a "set-it-and-forget-it" model. Meet with a financial professional at least yearly to address any changes and revisit your retirement planning checklist to make sure you're still on track.

**Tax Efficiency**

• Revisit your spending projections at the start of each year. Are you drawing down from accounts in the most tax-efficient order? Has inflation or lifestyle shifted your needs? Are you maintaining a sustainable withdrawal rate?

# Unintended Consequences

One of the most vital insights I uncovered during my own planning is that financial moves in retirement always carry unintended consequences. What seems like an excellent strategy in one area of your portfolio can trigger a devastating domino effect in another.

To understand why, you have to look at retirement as a machine with five interconnected financial gears:

1. **Pre-65 Healthcare:** Navigating the ACA Marketplace, COBRA, or retiree company health plans.
2. **Medicare:** Transitioning to federal healthcare at age 65.
3. **Social Security:** Strategizing your filing age anywhere between 62 and 70.
4. **Pensions, Annuities and other income:** Managing predictable, fixed lifetime distributions as well as other income streams.
5. **Traditional IRAs & 401(k)s:** Controlling the timing and size of taxable distributions.

Here is how those gears collide: If you retire early and rely on the Affordable Care Act (ACA) Marketplace for health insurance, your monthly premiums are based entirely on your Modified Adjusted Gross Income (MAGI). It does not matter how high your net worth is or how many millions you have sitting in bank accounts; the government only looks at your reportable income.

Because the enhanced federal subsidies expired, the strict "subsidy cliff" is back. If your MAGI goes even one dollar over the limit, your premium tax credits vanish instantly. For the 2026 tax year, that hard cliff sits at **$84,600** for a married couple filing jointly and **$62,600** for a single filer.

To understand the incredibly high stakes of managing your MAGI before age 65, look at a real-world case study for an early retiree couple, both age 62, living in Georgia.

Because health insurance premiums scale significantly with age, unsubsidized retail rates for individuals in their early 60s are at their absolute peak. In Georgia, the average full-retail cost for a benchmark Silver marketplace plan for a 62-year-old couple is approximately $2,200 per month—a staggering **$26,400 annually**.

Here is exactly how the ACA contribution scale slides based on a household size of two (using the baseline 100% FPL of $21,150), and the exact monthly and annual consequences of crossing each threshold.

### The ACA Contribution Scale Breakdown (GA Age-62 Couple)

| FPL Tier & MAGI Level | Max Premium % Cap | What the Couple Pays (Monthly) | What the Couple Pays (Annual) | Monthly Subsidy Received |
|---|---|---|---|---|
| **150% FPL** ($31,725) | ~4.00% of income | **$106** | **$1,269** | $2,094 |
| **200% FPL** ($42,300) | ~6.30% of income | **$222** | **$2,665** | $1,978 |
| **250% FPL** ($52,875) | ~8.05% of income | **$355** | **$4,256** | $1,845 |
| **300% FPL** ($63,450) | 9.96% of income | **$527** | **$6,320** | $1,673 |
| **399% FPL** ($84,400) *Just Under Cliff* | 9.96% of income | **$701** | **$8,406** | $1,499 |
| **401% FPL** ($84,401+) | **No Cap (0% Subsidy)** | **$2,200** | **$26,400** | **$0** |

# Step-by-Step Financial Consequences

## 1. Shifting Between Safe Tiers (Gradual Increases)

Within the boundaries of the 100% to 400% FPL zone, increases in your MAGI cause your premium to rise, but the changes are predictable and progressive:

- **Moving from 150% to 200% FPL:** If an extra investment distribution bumps income from $31,725 to $42,300, the monthly premium increases by **$116/month** ($1,396/year).
- **Moving from 250% to 300% FPL:** Bumping income from $52,875 to $63,450 increases the premium by **$172/month** ($2,064/year).

## 2. The Danger Zone: Crossing the 400% FPL "Subsidy Cliff"

The catastrophic financial consequence occurs at the final threshold. Because the expanded subsidy rules have expired, crossing 400% FPL ($84,600 for a couple) removes the protective premium cap entirely.

- **Scenario A (Managed MAGI - $84,400):** The couple carefully calculates their income, capping it just under the threshold. They pay **$701 per month** ($8,406/year). The federal government picks up the remaining $1,499 per month via tax credits.
- **Scenario B (Unmanaged MAGI - $84,800):** The couple takes an extra $400 out of a Traditional IRA or triggers a small capital gain. Their income ticks up to $84,800—just $200 past the legal cliff line.

## The Difference:

- **Monthly Penalty:** Out-of-pocket premium costs immediately jump from $701 to $2,200. An extra **$1,499 per month**.
- **Annual Penalty:** Total healthcare costs spike from $8,406 to $26,400. An extra **$17,994 per year**.

Because of a tiny $400 oversight in income tracking, this Georgia couple loses **$17,994** in purchasing power.

## The Strategic Lesson

This illustrates why early retirees must ruthlessly control their MAGI.

If this couple needs an extra $20,000 in cash during the year to replace a roof or fund a trip, pulling that $20,000 from a **Traditional IRA** triggers the $18,000 cliff penalty (effectively costing them $38,000 for a $20,000 expense).

Pulling that same $20,000 from a **Roth IRA** or a tax-free **return of principal from a non-qualified annuity** keeps their MAGI locked perfectly at the $701/month tier.

Or having cash on hand for these large purchases or emergencies will not impact your MAGI.

# Medicare Consequences

When most people turn 65, Medicare is the go to place for their health care coverage. Your MAGI will determine what you pay for Medicare. When you see the example you will see how the surcharge/penalty/tax impacts you.

The government may call it a surcharge, but I call it a penalty and or a tax! You need to think in those terms and how you can reduce, minimize or eliminate these!

Just like the ACA marketplace, the Medicare IRMAA system relies on strict income thresholds. However, IRMAA has a unique feature that amplifies the financial consequences for retirees: **it is a personal surcharge.**

If you are married and both you and your spouse are enrolled in Medicare, jumping over an IRMAA line means **both of you** are hit with the penalty. Your household costs do not just increase; they double.

Here is the exact mathematical breakdown of how the 2026 IRMAA surcharges stack up for a married couple filing jointly, and the real-world penalty of missing a cliff by a single dollar.

## The 2026 Married Couple IRMAA Surcharge Scale

*Note: These surcharges are paid* ***in addition*** *to your standard base Medicare Part B premium ($202.90/month) and whatever private Part D prescription drug plan premium you choose.*

| Surcharge Tier & Joint MAGI | Part B Surcharge (Per Person/Mo) | Part D Surcharge (Per Person/Mo) | Total Surcharge (Per Person/Mo) | Total Surcharge (Per Couple/Annual) |
|---|---|---|---|---|
| **Base Plan** ($218,000 or less) | $0.00 | $0.00 | $0.00 | **$0.00** |
| **Tier 1** ($218,001 to $274,000) | $81.20 | $14.50 | $95.70 | **$2,296.80** |
| **Tier 2** ($274,001 to $342,000) | $202.90 | $37.50 | $240.40 | **$5,769.60** |
| **Tier 3** ($342,001 to $410,000) | $324.60 | $60.40 | $385.00 | **$9,240.00** |
| **Tier 4** ($410,001 to $749,999) | $446.30 | $83.30 | $529.60 | **$12,710.40** |
| **Tier 5** ($750,000 or more) | $487.00 | $91.00 | $578.00 | **$13,872.00** |

# Step-by-Step Financial Consequences

## 1. The "First Dollar" Mistake (Base to Tier 1)

Assume a retired couple manages their income beautifully from their pensions and capital gains, projection-modelling their tax year to hit right at the top of the base tier.

- **Scenario A (Perfect Execution - $218,000 MAGI):** They pay exactly $0 in surcharges. Their collective Medicare premiums are just the standard base rates.
- **Scenario B (The $1 Oversight - $218,001 MAGI):** A surprise mutual fund dividend distributions triggers in December, pushing their joint MAGI up by one single dollar.

Because they stepped over the line, the federal government applies the Tier 1 surcharge to **both** individuals for all 12 months of the year.

- **Monthly Penalty:** Each person owes an extra $95.70 per month. Together, the couple faces a **$191.40 per month** cash flow drain.
- **Annual Penalty:** Over the course of the year, that single extra dollar of income costs the couple **$2,296.80** out of pocket.

## 2. The Deeper Retirement Jump (Tier 1 to Tier 2)

The cliffs become significantly steeper the higher your income climbs. Imagine a couple executing a massive Roth IRA conversion sequence to clean out their pre-tax accounts. They decide to push their income deep into Tier 1, targeting $274,000.

- **Scenario A (Managed Conversion - $274,000 MAGI):** The couple stays in Tier 1. Their combined annual IRMAA penalty is **$2,296.80**.
- **Scenario B (Unmanaged Conversion - $274,001 MAGI):** They miscalculate their interest income or capital gains by one dollar, logging a MAGI of $274,001.

They instantly land in Tier 2. The surcharge per person climbs from $95.70 to $240.40 per month.

- **The Marginal Difference:** Their combined annual surcharge vaults from $2,296.80 up to **$5,769.60**.

**The Penalty:** Crossing that specific boundary line by $1 results in a net loss of **$3,472.80** in retirement cash.

## The Strategic Lesson: The Tax Rate Illusion

When you calculate the math on these cliffs, you expose the true danger of unmanaged retirement income: **exorbitant hidden marginal tax rates.**

If you cross the Tier 1 to Tier 2 boundary by a single dollar, you are technically paying a **347,280% marginal tax rate** on that specific dollar of income ($3,472.80 in penalties divided by $1 of income).

To prevent these spikes, precise portfolio coordination is necessary:

1. **The 2-Year Lag Time:** Because 2026 premiums are based on 2024 tax returns, income adjustments must occur *two years in advance.* Your cash flow choices at age 63 establish what you will pay the day you turn 65.
2. **Tax-Free Spigots:** When a capital gain or a required minimum distribution (RMD) naturally threatens to push you toward the edge of an IRMAA bracket, any additional cash needed for lifestyle expenses, home maintenance, or travel should be intentionally pulled from **Roth IRAs**, cash savings, or **non-qualified annuity principal distributions** to prevent triggering the double-surcharge penalty.

Here is the vital lesson: exactly how much money you withdraw from your retirement accounts—and where you choose to pull it from—matters immensely. You must become a diligent student of how these rules apply to your specific situation so you don't get hit with unexpected surcharges, penalties, and taxes.

To put this into perspective, consider how interconnected your income streams truly are:

- **The ACA Subsidies Connection:** When you choose to claim Social Security, take a pension payout, or pull from a traditional IRA, you directly impact your income level. If you retire before age 65, this income can dramatically reduce your Affordable Care Act (ACA) health care subsidies.

- **The Medicare Premium Impact:** The amount you withdraw from Social Security, pensions, and IRAs later impacts what you will pay for Medicare. Crossing certain income thresholds triggers IRMAA (Income-Related Monthly Adjustment Amount) surcharges, drastically increasing your monthly premiums.

- **The Power of a "Cash Bridge":** Building a cash reserve before age 65 can help you safely navigate ACA marketplace subsidy cliffs. Because spending down cash does not increase your Modified Adjusted Gross Income (MAGI), it keeps your listed income low. For example, if you want to retire at age 62, having three years of cash to live on before transitioning to Medicare and claiming Social Security can save you thousands of dollars in health insurance premiums.

Ultimately, you should work closely with a qualified financial professional to map out your unique situation, ensuring you maximize your income while minimizing or eliminating unnecessary tax penalties.

# Power of Inflation

Below is a comparison showing how prices have changed from approximately 1990 to today (2025–2026). The figures are national averages or representative prices and are intended to illustrate the impact of inflation and rising costs over time.

**For context:** Overall U.S. inflation from 1990 to 2025 was about **146.5%**, meaning something costing $1.00 in 1990 would cost about **$2.47 today** if it simply tracked inflation.

## Key Comparisons That Tell the Story

| Item | 1990 Price | Today Price | Difference | % Change |
|---|---|---|---|---|
| **Median Home Price** | $123,000 | $420,000 | +$297,000 | +241% |
| **Average Monthly Rent** | $447 | $1,700 | +$1,253 | +280% |
| **Average New Car (all vehicles)** | $16,000 | $49,000 | +$33,000 | +206% |
| **First-Class Stamp** | $0.25 | $0.73 | +$0.48 | +192% |
| **Average Private College Tuition** | $9,300 | $43,000 | +$33,700 | +362% |
| **Public University Tuition (National Avg.)** | $1,780 | $11,600 | +$9,820 | +552% |

## 1990 vs Today: Cost of Living Comparison (USA)

| Item | 1990 Price | Today Price | Difference | % Change |
|---|---|---|---|---|
| **Gallon of Milk** | $2.15 | $4.20 | +$2.05 | +95% |
| **Loaf of Bread** | $0.69 | $1.93 | +$1.24 | +180% |
| **Dozen Eggs** | $1.01 | $4.95 | +$3.94 | +390% |
| **2-Liter Coke** | $0.99 | $2.99 | +$2.00 | +202% |
| **Bananas (per lb.)** | $0.33 | $0.69 | +$0.36 | +109% |
| **Gasoline (gallon)** | $1.15 | $3.21 | +$2.06 | +179% |
| **Starbucks Coffee (tall brewed)** | ~$0.85 | ~$3.25 | +$2.40 | +282% |
| **Movie Ticket** | $4.22 | $11.31 | +$7.09 | +168% |
| **McDonald's Big Mac** | $2.10 | $5.69 | +$3.59 | +171% |
| **Costco Membership** | $25 | $65 | +$40 | +160% |
| **Hamburger Meat (1 lb.)** | $1.55 | $5.49 | +$3.94 | +254% |
| **Disney World 1-Day Ticket** | $31 | $189 | +$158 | +510% |
| **Toyota Camry (new)** | $13,600 | $30,000 | +$16,400 | +121% |
| **Ford F-150 (new)** | $12,800 | $39,500 | +$26,700 | +209% |
| **University of Georgia Tuition (In-State)** | ~$1,600/year | ~$10,400/year | +$8,800 | +550% |

# Which Items Rose Faster Than Inflation?

Remember, inflation alone would have increased prices by about **146.5%** since 1990.

## Increased MUCH Faster Than Inflation

- University tuition (+550%)
- Disney World tickets (+510%)
- Eggs (+390%)
- Private college tuition (+362%)
- Rent (+280%)
- Hamburger meat (+254%)
- Housing (+241%)

## Roughly In Line With Inflation

- Gasoline (+179%)
- Movie tickets (+168%)
- Big Mac (+171%)
- Costco membership (+160%)

## Increased Less Than Overall Inflation

- Milk (+95%)
- Toyota Camry (+121%)

The biggest takeaway is that when you plan for retirement - you have to understand that inflation is REAL and reduces your purchasing power over time. In the next table, take a look at what happens to the price of things if we use general inflation method to calculate prices in the future.

# Projected Price Change by 2060

| Item | 1990 | Today (2025-26) | 2060 Projection | Increase 1990→2060 |
|---|---|---|---|---|
| Gallon of Milk | $2.15 | $4.20 | $10.35 | +381% |
| Loaf of Bread | $0.69 | $1.93 | $4.76 | +590% |
| Dozen Eggs | $1.01 | $4.95 | $12.20 | +1,108% |
| 2-Liter Coke | $0.99 | $2.99 | $7.37 | +644% |
| Bananas (per lb.) | $0.33 | $0.69 | $1.70 | +415% |
| Gasoline (gallon) | $1.15 | $3.21 | $7.91 | +588% |
| Starbucks Coffee | $0.85 | $3.25 | $8.01 | +842% |
| Movie Ticket | $4.22 | $11.31 | $27.88 | +561% |
| McDonald's Big Mac | $2.10 | $5.69 | $14.02 | +568% |
| Costco Membership | $25 | $65 | $160.23 | +541% |
| Hamburger Meat (1 lb.) | $1.55 | $5.49 | $13.53 | +773% |
| Disney World Ticket | $31 | $189 | $465.89 | +1,403% |
| Toyota Camry | $13,600 | $30,000 | $73,950 | +444% |
| Ford F-150 | $12,800 | $39,500 | $97,368 | +661% |
| UGA Tuition (In-State) | $1,600 | $10,400 | $25,636 | +1,502% |

| Item | 1990 | Today | 2060 Projection |
|---|---|---|---|
| Median Home Price | $123,000 | $420,000 | $1,035,300 |
| Average Monthly Rent | $447 | $1,700 | $4,191 |
| Average New Vehicle | $16,000 | $49,000 | $120,785 |
| First-Class Stamp | $0.25 | $0.73 | $1.80 |
| Private College Tuition | $9,300 | $43,000 | $105,995 |
| Public University Tuition (National Avg.) | $1,780 | $11,600 | $28,594 |

# What $100 Buys

This is often the most powerful inflation illustration:

| Year | Purchasing Power of $100 |
|---|---|
| **1990** | $100 |
| **2025** | $40.57 |
| **2060 (if trend repeats)** | $16.46 |

In other words:

- $100 in 1990 buys roughly what **$247** buys today.
- $100 in 1990 would buy roughly what **$609** buys in 2060.
- A person retiring in 2060 may need about **6 times as many dollars** to maintain the same lifestyle that $100 provided in 1990.

If the next 35 years resemble the last 35 years, overall prices could more than double again by 2060. A $420,000 home becomes a $1.0 million home, a $30,000 car becomes a $74,000 car, and a $5.69 Big Mac becomes a $14 meal item—not because the products necessarily change, but because the purchasing power of the dollar continues to decline over time.

Inflation is not an abstract idea or thought. It is real, and you have to plan for the eventuality when you think about your retirement savings.

# Power of Compounding

*"Compound interest is the eighth wonder of the world. He who understands it, earns it; he who doesn't, pays it."* **Albert Einstein**

**Time plus compounding interest is truly a powerful force**. The sooner you start, the sooner your money begins working for you. Ultimately, the goal at the end of your working life is to have your investments doing the heavy lifting.

If you consistently save money—whether weekly, bi-weekly, or monthly—your portfolio will inevitably grow. Saving is a habit, much like exercise: the more you work out, the stronger you get; the more you save, the more financial security you build.

## Benjamin Franklin Example

When Benjamin Franklin passed away in 1790, he was already famous for his maxims on thrift, such as his classic reminder that "a penny saved is a penny earned." However, his greatest demonstration of this principle didn't occur during his lifetime. Instead, it was engineered through a unique, multi-century experiment written directly into his last will and testament.

Spurred in part by a French mathematician who had mocked his unrelenting American optimism, Franklin decided to prove that small, disciplined savings could organically multiply into an absolute fortune.

# The Strategic Experiment: A 200-Year Codicil

In a codicil (an amendment) to his will, Franklin bequeathed **1,000 pounds sterling** (roughly $4,444 at the time) to two cities he cherished: **Boston**, his birthplace, and **Philadelphia**, his adopted home. Rather than allowing the cities to spend the money immediately, Franklin attached strict strings to the capital, structuring a two-tiered timeline designed to harness the raw physics of compounding interest.

# A Tale of Two Cities: The Divergent Results

When the experiment officially concluded two centuries later in 1990, the real-world results beautifully demonstrated both the staggering power and the operational vulnerabilities of long-term investing.

Because of changing economic landscapes, the rise of industrial factories (which reduced the pool of traditional solo apprentices), and occasional defaults or management differences, the funds did not hit Franklin's exact mathematical projections. However, they still yielded millions:

- **Boston's Strategy:** Boston opted to minimize risk and ultimately shifted a significant portion of its capital into broader, long-term trust investments. By the early 1990s, Boston's fund had grown to roughly **$4.5 million**. The city used its intermediate and final windfalls to support civic causes and fund the Franklin Institute of Boston (now the Benjamin Franklin Cummings Institute of Technology).
- **Philadelphia's Strategy:** Philadelphia adhered more strictly to Franklin's original intent of prioritizing direct loans to individuals. Due to economic shifts and periods where finding qualified borrowers proved difficult, their capital spent more time sitting idle. Philadelphia's fund closed out at approximately **$2 million**, which helped establish the Franklin Institute science museum and continues to support scholarships for students entering the trades.

In total, Franklin's original combined investment of about $8,888 morphed into a legacy worth over **$6.5 million**. It remains one of the most brilliant, historic proofs that patience, structure, and time are the ultimate wealth multipliers.

# Cup of Coffee

Let's assume you buy a $5.50 cup of coffee every work day. Over 40 years, that adds up to roughly $62,400 spent on a beverage you could have brewed at home for less than $0.50 a cup.

If you had invested that daily coffee money instead—earning a conservative 3.75 % interest over those same 40 years—you would have nearly **$125,000.**

You can apply this exact same exercise to streaming services and the other small expenses that quietly sift through your fingers: Amazon, Netflix, Hulu, Disney+, Apple TV, Paramount+, ESPN+, YouTube, and Spotify.

The lesson is simple: start saving early, save often, and don't stop.

Remember, you can borrow money for a house or a car, but you cannot borrow money for retirement. You also cannot gamble your future on an inheritance or Social Security. Ultimately, your retirement is your responsibility.

# Power of Time

*"Time is your friend, impulse is your enemy. Take advantage of compound interest..."* **Warren Buffett**

Here is a fun story to demonstrate the power of time!

## The Unfair Advantage of Time

Elena and Marcus walked into the same engineering firm on the exact same Monday in July, fresh out of college at age 22. Both started with a $50,000 salary, and both could expect a modest 2.5% annual raise over their careers.

But their philosophies on money couldn't have been more different.

To Elena, money was a tool to buy future independence. To Marcus, money was a tool to enjoy the present. Neither was inherently wrong, but only one of them understood the hidden physics of wealth.

### Elena's Path: The 20-Year Sprint

Elena decided right away to automate her savings. She chose a boring, middle-of-the-road approach: putting **10% of her salary** into her retirement account every single month. In her first year, that was $5,000. As her salary grew by 2.5% each year, her contribution grew right along with it. She invested in a diversified portfolio that averaged a historically reasonable **7% annual return**.

Elena kept this up for exactly 20 years. At age 42, facing a comfortable mid-career shift and new life priorities, she made a radical choice: **she stopped**

**contributing entirely.** For the next 20 years, from age 42 to 62, she didn't add a single penny of her own money. She just left it alone.

# Marcus's Path: The 20-Year Delay

Marcus wanted to live a little first. He figured, "*I'm young, my salary is low, and I have plenty of time. I'll catch up later when I'm making the big bucks.*" For the first 20 years of his career, Marcus saved exactly $0 for retirement. He drove nicer cars, took memorable vacations, and didn't stress about tomorrow.

Then came their 42nd year.

Over a casual lunch, Elena mentioned offhand that she was turning off her retirement contributions because her nest egg was already self-sustaining. Intrigued and slightly panicked, Marcus went home that night and finally opened a retirement calculator.

The realization hit him like a physical blow. He was completely broke, while Elena's account was already hurtling toward a fortune. Determined to catch up by their 62nd birthdays, Marcus committed to saving whatever it took.

# The Cold Math of Catching Up

To match the massive head start Elena's money got from two decades of compounding, Marcus didn't just have to save what Elena saved—he had to make up for the *time* his money lost.

Assuming the exact same 7% market return, here is how the numbers shake out by the time they both reach **age 62**:

## The Final Scoreboard

- **Elena's Total Out-of-Pocket Contribution:** Over her 20 years of saving, Elena contributed a total of **$127,720**. Thanks to the power of time, by age 62, her account has snowballed into roughly **$835,000**.
- **Marcus's Required Catch-Up Effort:** To hit that exact same $835,000 target by age 62, Marcus cannot just save 10%. He can't even just save

20%. Marcus has to save roughly **27.5% of his salary** every single year for the next 20 years.

- **Marcus's Total Out-of-Pocket Contribution:** Because he compressed his savings window, Marcus has to write checks totalling roughly **$431,000** out of his own pocket to land in the same place.

## The Secret Ingredient: The Invisible Employee

Why did Elena win so effortlessly? Because by year 20, she had hired an **Invisible Employee** inside her account.

When you invest early, compound interest stops being a math concept and becomes a functioning worker. By the time Elena was 42, her accumulated nest egg was generating more growth in a single year through market returns than she was putting in from her pay check. When she stopped saving, her Invisible Employee stayed on the clock, working 24/7 for the next 20 years, entirely for free.

Marcus, on the other hand, had no such help. Because he started at zero at age 42, he had to do all the heavy lifting himself. He didn't have an army of past dollars working for him; he only had his current, hard-earned pay check.

## The Mid-Life Lifestyle Squeeze

The numbers tell the financial story, but the human story happens in the budget.

Think about what occurs at age 42. This is typically the most expensive phase of a person's life. You might be paying a hefty mortgage, raising teenagers, dealing with soaring healthcare costs, or supporting aging parents.

- **Elena's Reality:** At age 42, Elena freed up 10% of her income. She could redirect that money to a child's college fund, pay down her mortgage early, or take her family on vacations without ever jeopardizing her retirement. Her future was already bought and paid for.

- **Marcus's Reality:** At age 42, Marcus had to *slash* his take-home pay by nearly **30%**. Imagine trying to raise a family and manage a household while instantly giving up almost a third of your pay check just to avoid poverty in old age. The psychological strain on Marcus was immense. He was constantly stressed, cutting corners, and feeling the suffocating guilt of his early delays.

## The Exponential Cost of Waiting

The ultimate lesson of Elena and Marcus is that the "Cost of Delay" is not a flat fee—it is an exponential penalty.

Waiting 20 years to save didn't mean Marcus had to save twice as much. It meant he had to contribute **more than three times as much out of his own pocket** and sacrifice a massive chunk of his peak earning years just to cross the finish line neck-and-neck with Elena.

Elena paid a small, manageable toll during her youth. Marcus paid a devastating, high-interest tax during his prime.

**The Late-Stage Tax Impact:** There is an even crueller twist to Marcus's strategy. By trying to shove $431,000 into retirement accounts in his 40s and 50s, Marcus will smash right into IRS contribution limits. He won't even be able to hide all of this money in tax-advantaged accounts like a standard 401(k), forcing him to invest some in taxable accounts—meaning Uncle Sam will take an extra cut of his late-stage hustle, making his uphill climb even steeper.

Time can be your friend, or it can be your enemy. Ultimately, how you choose to use it is what matters.

Time is one of the most precious commodities on Earth. Once it has passed, it cannot be reclaimed; it is gone forever. It does not matter if you are rich or poor—everyone receives the exact same twenty-four hours each day. Choose to use your time wisely.

**BTW - If we had considered that their employer offered a 5% company match to 401K savings, then Elena would have been closer to $1,500,000!!**

# Epilogue

## Epilogue: Crossing Your Own Finish Line

Well, friend, we have spent a lot of time talking about the numbers, the rules, the dates, and the common pitfalls. We have looked at the hard-earned wisdom of hundreds of people, who took this path before us—some who tripped over the hidden tripwires, and others who sailed through with a smile. But when you close this book, the spread sheets fade away. What you are left with isn't a math problem. It is your life.

Retirement is the ultimate plot twist. For forty or fifty years, you knew exactly who you were when you woke up in the morning. You were a worker, a provider, a saver, and a person with a title. You built your whole life around a calendar that someone else mostly controlled. Then, one day, the engine stops. The daily rush vanishes. You get handed your freedom on a silver platter, and suddenly, you are the captain of an empty ship with an endless ocean ahead of you.

That transition messes with your head. It is a beautiful, terrifying, and deeply weird experience. There is a proverb that says "*He who specifies his destination can find his path, but he who has nowhere to go is truly lost.*" If you do not have a vision for what you are running toward, you will quickly find that an endless vacation gets boring fast.

### The Wisdom of All Ages

This book isn't just for the folks who are packing up their desks this afternoon. It is a roadmap for every single adult turning a page in their own story.

- **For the 20-Something and 30-Something Dreamers:** You might look at a book about retirement and think it belongs to a different planet. But the single biggest regret shared by seniors is that they simply did not start saving early enough. Time is the only financial asset you cannot buy back. When you save early, compounding growth does the heavy lifting so you do not have to break your back later.

- **For the 40-Something Achievers:** The reality of youth is fading and you realize you are the adult in the room now. Responsibility is real and now retirement is no a completely abstract idea, but an actual event that you need to prepare for suffer the consequences. It is not too late to start saving or develop a retirement plan!
- **For the 50-Something Hustlers:** You are hitting the peak of your career and the peak of your earnings. This is your yellow flag context. It is time to look at your portfolio, grab those government "catch-up" bonuses, and start figuring out what your life looks like when the pay checks stop hitting your bank account.
- **For the 70-Something and 80-Something Sages:** Your job now is significance, not just success. It is about sharing the stories, keeping your body moving, avoiding the isolation trap, and loving your people with every single ounce of energy you have left.

## An Anecdote on True Wealth

John spent 35 years working a high-stress corporate job, earning the absolute maximum salary he could manage. He checked his balances every single hour. He was a champion saver. On the day he turned 60, he packed his boxes, walked out of the building, and bought a massive, top-of-the-line luxury motorhome. He told everyone he was going to see every square inch of America.

Two years later, the giant motorhome was parked in his driveway, covered in dust. John looked exhausted. A friend asked him how the great American road trip was going.

He smiled a little sadly and said, "You know what I realized? The motorhome didn't make me happy. It just introduced double the maintenance costs and gave me a larger windshield to clean.

"I was so busy checking off boxes on a bucket list that I forgot to ask who I was actually traveling with. My wife and I were in each other's hair twenty-four hours a day without any personal space. My knees started acting up from all the driving, and I realized I had left all my real neighborhood friends back home just to sit in empty parking lots."

John had fallen straight into the classic retirement traps: the identity crisis, the spousal friction, the physical neglect, and the lifestyle miscalculation. He focused so heavily on building a giant nest egg that he forgot to build a life that could fit inside it.

## Turning the Mess into a Success

The golden secret to getting retirement right is simple: you have to move from a mindset of hoarding to a mindset of experiencing. My natural tendency throughout my entire adult life was to save, save, and save some more.

Giving myself permission to actually spend the money I worked so hard to accumulate was terrifying. But the retirees who are genuinely happy are the ones who front-load their big adventures during their active "Go-Go" years before their joints and energy levels force them to slow down.

You also have to remember that your health is your real bank account. You can have all the money in the world at Vanguard or any other financial house, but if your body cannot get down on the floor to play with your grandkids, your wealth is essentially useless. Consistency, kindness to your joints, daily walks, and drinking enough water are non-negotiable duties if you want to keep your freedom.

Finally, do not walk this path alone. Keep your spouse or your partner close. Communicate your fears, give each other space to breathe, and share the keys to the financial kingdom so nobody is left in the dark. Reach out to your neighbors, help a friend who can no longer drive, and make your home a warm harbor for the people you love.

Retirement isn't the end of your story. It is the beginning of your second act. Make it intentional, keep it honest, laugh at the popping joints, and choose to finish well.

# Summary

## The Roadmap — From Retirement Mess to Retirement Success

Congratulations—you have made it to the final destination. If you only read one chapter of this book, or if you need a quick, no-nonsense refresher before making your next big financial move, this summary is designed to give you a comprehensive, bird's-eye view of everything required to transition from a "retirement mess" into a "retirement success".

Retirement is not a one-size-fits-all equation. It requires you to become a dedicated student of your own wealth, lifestyle, and longevity. What follows is the definitive cheat sheet of the milestones, math, regrets, and mechanics detailed throughout this book.

## 1. The Core Philosophy: Shifting from Saving to Spending

For over 40 years, your natural financial instinct has likely been to save, save, save. The hardest psychological hurdle in retirement is turning off that accumulation engine and learning how to spend your nest egg. Three core lessons anchor this book's philosophy:

- **Capitalize on the "Go-Go" Years:** Travel and pursue physically demanding bucket-list adventures while you are still young and agile enough to enjoy them.
- **Spend More Early:** Do not hoard all your wealth until the end of your life. Invest in experiences and create core memories early in your retirement journey.
- **Retire With Purpose:** Retirement isn't just about escaping a job; it's about running toward a purpose, whether that is writing, mentoring, or starting a passion project.

## 2. The Critical Chronological Milestones

Missing a single age milestone can result in permanent government penalties or missed wealth-building opportunities. Keep this timeline permanently bookmarked:

### The Accumulation Phase (Ages 20 to 49)

- **20s, 30s, & 40s:** Consistently save a target of 15% of your income from every single pay check and maximize employer matching programs.

### The Acceleration Phase (Ages 50 to 59)

- **Age 50:** Conduct a portfolio risk review to prevent catastrophic late-stage market losses. Begin utilizing government "catch-up contributions" (in 2026, this allows an extra $8,000 for 401(k)s and $1,100 for IRAs).
- **Age 55:** You qualify for an additional $1,000 annual HSA catch-up contribution. This is also the first age you can access current workplace retirement funds penalty-free via the **Rule of 55** if you separate from service.
- **Age 59½:** The standard 10% early withdrawal penalty on traditional IRAs and retirement accounts officially expires.

### The Optimization Phase (Ages 60 to 70+)

- **Age 62:** The earliest age to claim Social Security, but it comes with a **permanent lifestyle penalty**—a 30% reduction in your monthly benefit if your full retirement age is 67.
- **Age 63:** The Medicare "Look-back" age. The government examines your Modified Adjusted Gross Income (MAGI) from this year to determine your future healthcare premiums.
- **Age 65:** Your initial Medicare enrollment window opens (a 7-month bracket around your birthday). Missing this window triggers lifetime premium penalties of 10% per year for Part B and 1% per month for Part D.

- **Age 67:** Full Retirement Age (FRA) for anyone born in 1960 or later, unlocking 100% of your baseline Social Security benefits.
- **Age 70:** Your Social Security benefits hit their absolute maximum, locking in a permanent 24% delayed retirement bonus. There is zero financial incentive to wait past your 70th birthday.
- **Age 70½:** You become eligible for **Qualified Charitable Distributions (QCDs)**, letting you transfer up to $111,000 annually (in 2026) directly from an IRA to a charity completely tax-free.
- **Ages 73 to 75: Required Minimum Distributions (RMDs)** kick in based on your birth year (Age 73 if born 1951–1959; Age 75 if born 1960 or later). Failing to take your mandated RMD triggers a harsh 25% tax penalty.

# 3. The Rules of Wealth: Compounding and Time

Time is the ultimate financial multiplier. The book illustrates this using three core examples:

- **The Invisible Employee:** Through the case study of Elena (who saved from ages 22 to 42 and stopped) and Marcus (who delayed saving until age 42), we see the brutal cost of delay. Elena accumulated $835,000 by age 62 out-of-pocketing only $127,720 because her "invisible employee" (compound interest) worked for her 24/7. Marcus had to save 27.5% of his salary and spend $431,000 out-of-pocket just to reach the exact same finish line.
- **The Historic Proof:** Benjamin Franklin's famous 200-year multi-century experiment proved that a small initial gift of roughly $8,888 to Boston and Philadelphia multiplied into a civic legacy worth over $6.5 million through pure patience and time.
- **Daily Financial Leaks:** Buying a $5.50 cup of coffee every workday over 40 years sifts $62,400 through your fingers. Invested at a conservative 3.75% interest rate instead, that daily coffee habit transforms into nearly $125,000.

## 4. The 13 Greatest Retiree Regrets

To avoid a retirement mess, you must actively steer clear of the primary pitfalls identified by senior citizens who crossed the finish line before you:

1. Not saving enough money or starting to save soon enough.
2. Not pulling the trigger and retiring sooner.
3. Failing to understand complex retirement taxes, cliffs, and penalties.
4. Operating without a formal financial plan or refusing to consult experts.
5. Lacking a clear purpose or daily schedule for how time will actually be spent.
6. Neglecting physical health and fitness during peak working years.
7. Failing to invest deep, intentional time into key family relationships.
8. Unwise spending on rapidly depreciating, big-ticket luxury items.
9. Excluding a spouse or partner from the primary retirement planning conversations.
10. Delaying or entirely abandoning personal passion projects and creative ideas.
11. Not traveling when physical health was at its absolute peak.
12. Failing to fully maximize the high-energy "Go-Go" years of early retirement.
13. Failing to switch from a saving to a spending mindset, resulting in hoarding money.

## 5. The Ultimate Toolbox: 14 Retirement Calculation Methods

When determining if you have saved enough to sustain your future, the financial world offers several competing methodologies. A successful plan often uses a combination of these frameworks:

| **Strategy / Method** | **Core Operational Mechanics** | **Primary Benefit / Downside** |
|---|---|---|
| **Salary Multipliers** | Targets savings landmarks based on age milestones (1x salary at 30, 3x at 40, 6x at 50, 8x at 60, 10-11x at 67). | **Pro:** Quick, simple benchmark.<br><br>**Con:** Blind to actual individual expenses. |
| **The 4% Rule** | Withdraw 4% of your total portfolio in Year 1, then adjust that static dollar amount strictly for inflation every year after. | **Pro:** Extreme simplicity, battle-tested.<br><br>**Con:** Vulnerable to early Sequence of Returns Risk. |
| **The 25x Expense Rule** | Multiply your net annual retirement expenses (total budget minus guaranteed income) by 25 to find your target nest egg. | **Pro:** Mathematical twin of the 4% rule.<br><br>**Con:** Treats all accounts as tax-equal. |
| **70% to 80% Income Replacement** | Models your retirement budget around replacing a vast majority of your final pre-retirement gross career salary. | **Pro:** Excellent for early/mid-career estimates.<br><br>**Con:** Actively penalizes high savers. |

| Strategy / Method | Core Operational Mechanics | Primary Benefit / Downside |
|---|---|---|
| **The Early Retirement 30x–33x Rule** | Accumulate 30x to 33x your net annual expenses, dropping your safe withdrawal rate to a highly conservative 3%. | **Pro:** Practically eliminates half-century longevity risk.<br><br>**Con:** Can cause severe career burnout. |
| **Capital Preservation (Yield-Only)** | Shift your allocation to fixed income, CDs, and dividend stocks; live strictly off interest without ever touching the principal. | **Pro:** Total immunity from sequence risk; ideal for heirs.<br><br>**Con:** Vulnerable to long-term inflation erosion. |
| **Expense-Based Blueprint** | Conduct a granular, line-item audit of your real-world anticipated fixed and variable retirement costs. | **Pro:** Highly accurate; prevents over-saving.<br><br>**Con:** Requires significant tracking effort. |

| Strategy / Method | Core Operational Mechanics | Primary Benefit / Downside |
|---|---|---|
| **Hybrid Bucket & Guardrail Strategy** | Divide assets into near, mid, and long-term buckets while applying Guyton-Klinger rules to cut or raise spending by 10%. | **Pro:** Strong behavioral armor against panic selling.<br><br>**Con:** Creates operational complexity and cash drag. |
| **Die With Zero** | Maximize lifetime fulfillment by intentionally liquidating assets to zero by your death; prioritize experiences and give inheritances early. | **Pro:** Aligns spending directly with your health-span.<br><br>**Con:** High risk if you unexpectedly outlive your plan. |
| **Vanguard Dynamic Spending** | Apply a strict ceiling (+5%) and floor (-2.5%) boundary system around a standard fixed-percentage annual withdrawal. | **Pro:** Drastically lowers probability of going broke.<br><br>**Con:** Requires annual manual recalibration. |

| Strategy / Method | Core Operational Mechanics | Primary Benefit / Downside |
|---|---|---|
| **Safety-First Approach** | Fund 100% of absolute essential expenses with secure contracts (Social Security, annuities, TIPS) and invest the rest for upside. | **Pro:** Complete peace of mind; independent of Wall Street.<br><br>**Con:** Requires sacrificing significant liquid capital. |
| **IRS Life Expectancy Method** | Look up your age on the IRS Uniform Lifetime Table annually and divide your portfolio by the matching shrinking divisor. | **Pro:** Mathematically impossible to run out of money.<br><br>**Con:** Annual income fluctuates wildly with the market. |
| **HECM Buffer Strategy** | Open a Home Equity Conversion Mortgage (reverse mortgage) line of credit to use as tax-free income during bear markets. | **Pro:** Insulates your core stock portfolio from down years.<br><br>**Con:** Expensive closing costs; eats home equity. |

| Strategy / Method | Core Operational Mechanics | Primary Benefit / Downside |
|---|---|---|
| **Monte Carlo Simulations** | Stress-test your specific asset allocation against 1,000+ randomized historical market sequences. | **Pro:** Replaces single flat guesses with real probability.<br><br>**Con:** Requires specialized software and tracking. |

---

# Final Words of Wisdom

The ultimate secret to a successful retirement is simple: **Become a student of retirement.** Do your own research, assemble a trusted team of licensed professionals (CFPs, CPAs, Lawyers and Physicians), and execute your plan with intentionality. Your retirement belongs uniquely to you—make it a masterpiece, not a mess.

# Terms and Acronyms

Retirement planning can quickly become overwhelming due to the sheer volume of financial jargon and acronyms. To help you navigate the landscape, I have created a foundational cheat sheet of the most critical terms you will encounter.

While this list is not exhaustive, it provides clear, high-level descriptions of the essentials. Consider this your starting point; you will want to conduct deeper research into how these rules specifically apply to your household. Please keep in mind that these definitions, thresholds, and regulations are constantly evolving as federal laws are updated and revised.

## Retirement Glossary (A to Z)

### 401(k) / 403(b)/ 457B/TSP

These are retirement savings plans offered by employers (your boss). A **401(k)** is used by regular businesses, while a **403(b)** is used by non-profits like schools or hospitals. You choose to automatically lower your current pay check by a little bit to put money into this account, where it grows over time. Often, employers will match a portion of whatever you put in—which is basically free money.

**457(b):** A tax-advantaged deferred-compensation retirement plan available for state and local government employees, as well as some tax-exempt organizations.

**TSP (Thrift Savings Plan):** A highly popular, low-fee retirement savings and investment plan for federal employees and members of the uniformed services.

## (ACA) Affordable Care Act Marketplace - "Obamacare"

Is essentially a regulated comparison-shopping platform for private health insurance. It's designed for anyone who needs major medical coverage but doesn't get it through a traditional corporate employer, Medicare, or Medicaid

## AGI (Adjusted Gross Income)

- **What it is:** Think of this as your "starting line" income for federal income taxes. It is your total income for the year minus a few specific, everyday discounts that the government lets you take right away.
- **What goes into it:**
    - *Income Added:* Everything you earn, including your job wages (W-2), business earnings, bank interest, stock dividends, capital gains (profit from selling an asset), and retirement account payouts.
    - *Deductions Subtracted:* Specific "above-the-line" items like money you put into a Health Savings Account (HSA), traditional IRA contributions, student loan interest payments, and classroom supplies paid for by school teachers.

## Annuity

Think of an annuity as a "reverse life insurance" contract. You give an insurance company a big chunk of money today, and in return, they promise to pay you a steady, guaranteed check every single month for the rest of your life (or for a set number of years) once you retire.

## Catch-Up Contributions

Once workers turn **50 years old**, the government lets them hit the accelerator on their savings. They are allowed to put extra money into their retirement accounts (above the normal legal limit) to "catch up" if they feel they haven't saved enough yet.

## CFP (Certified Financial Planner)

Think of a CFP as a personal trainer for your wallet. Instead of just picking individual stocks, they look at your whole financial life—your savings, insurance, taxes, and future dreams—and build a complete master plan to help you reach retirement safely. They have to pass a massive exam and are legally required to put your financial interests ahead of their own profits.

## COLA (Cost-of-Living Adjustment)

As time goes on, things get more expensive due to **inflation** (the general rise in prices over time). COLA is an automatic boost given to government benefits, like Social Security, to make sure retirees can still afford the same amount of groceries and rent even when prices go up.

## CPA (Certified Public Accountant)

A CPA is a super-powered accountant who has passed incredibly tough state exams to become a licensed tax master. While standard accountants can do basic math, a CPA knows the tax laws inside and out. In retirement, you hire them to help you figure out the legal strategies to pay the absolute lowest amount of money to the government when you start spending your savings.

## Defined Benefit Plan (Pension)

This is an old-school retirement plan where your employer promises to pay you a set, predictable amount of money every single month after you retire. The amount is usually based on how many years you worked there and how much money you made. Traditional pensions are rare today; most companies have replaced them with 401(k)s.

## Defined Contribution Plan

This is the modern style of retirement plan (like a 401(k) or IRA). Instead of promising you a specific payout when you retire, you "contribute" a certain amount of money into the account now, invest it, and hope it grows. What you end up with at retirement depends entirely on how much you saved and how well your investments performed.

## FICA (Federal Insurance Contributions Act)

If you look at a pay check stub, you'll see money taken out for FICA. This is a mandatory federal tax that takes a small bite out of your income while you're working to fund two massive programs for older Americans: **Social Security** and **Medicare**.

## FIRE (Financial Independence, Retire Early)

This is a popular lifestyle movement where people try to save a massive chunk of their income (sometimes 50% to 70%) while they are young. The goal is to build up enough investments so they never *have* to work again, allowing them to retire in their 30s or 40s instead of their 60s.

## FPL (Federal Poverty Level)

The **Federal Poverty Level (FPL)**—officially referred to by the government as the **HHS Poverty Guidelines**—is an administrative measure of the minimum baseline income required for an individual or a household to cover essential daily living expenses (such as food, shelter, utilities, and clothing) in the United States.

It is issued every January by the **U.S. Department of Health and Human Services (HHS)** under the authority of the Omnibus Budget Reconciliation Act of 1981.

## FRA (Full Retirement Age)

The exact age you become eligible to receive full, unreduced Social Security benefits. Depending on your birth year, this ranges from age 66 to 67.

## HSA (Health Savings Account)

A special medical piggy bank. You put money into it tax-free to pay for doctor visits or medicine. The cool trick is that if you don't spend it, the money rolls over year after year. Once you turn 65, you can withdraw any leftover money for *anything* you want, making it a secret weapon for retirement savings. You must have a high deductible health plan to make deposits into an HSA.

## IRA (Individual Retirement Account)

Unlike a 401(k) which you get through a boss, an IRA is a retirement account you open completely on your own through a bank or investment app. It gives you special tax breaks to encourage you to save your money for old age.

## IRMAA (Income-Related Monthly Adjustment Amount)

Pronounced "ER-mah," this is an extra charge added to your Medicare health insurance bill. If you make a high income in retirement, the government decides you can afford to pay more for your healthcare. The most important thing to know is that IRMAA is a "cliff"—if you earn even one dollar over the limit, your monthly bill instantly jumps up by a massive amount.

## Investment Policy Statement (IPS)

An Investment Policy Statement is simply a written rulebook that outlines how you will manage your money. It does not have to be a long, boring document filled with fancy legal words. In fact, for most regular people, a single page is plenty.

Think of it as a contract you sign with yourself while you are calm, relaxed, and thinking clearly. It states exactly what your long-term goals are, how much risk you are willing to take, and exactly what types of investments you will use to get there.

### MAGI (Modified Adjusted Gross Income)

- **What it is:** This is your AGI with a slight twist. The government takes your AGI number and adds back a few of the deductions you just subtracted. They use this specific number to decide if you make too much money to qualify for certain tax perks.
- **What goes into it:**
    - *The Starting Number:* Your **AGI**.
    - *Items Added Back:* The student loan interest deduction you took earlier, any foreign earned income you excluded from your taxes, and tax-exempt interest earned from municipal bonds.

## Medicare

The federal government's health insurance program specifically designed for people aged **65 and older**. Since health insurance can be incredibly expensive when people get older and stop working, Medicare helps cover their hospital visits and doctor appointments.

## Nest Egg

A casual slang term for the total amount of money you have saved up and put aside for your retirement. Just like a bird carefully guards its nest egg until it hatches, workers guard and grow their savings until they retire.

## QCD (Qualified Charitable Distribution)

This is a special tax shortcut for giving money to charity. Usually, when you pull money out of a Traditional IRA, the government taxes you on it. But if you are **70½ or older**, the government lets you send money *directly* from your IRA to a charity. Because the money goes straight to the charity without hitting your bank account, you don't owe any taxes on it, and it even counts toward your yearly required withdrawal limit.

## Retirement Cliffs

In financial planning, a "cliff" is a rule where crossing a specific line by even one dollar completely flips your situation. For example, if you earn just $1 over an income limit, you might instantly lose a giant tax break or trigger a massive jump in your Medicare bills (like the IRMAA cliff). It's called a cliff because there is no smooth ramp—you go straight over the edge into a much more expensive category.

## Retirement Penalties

These are financial punishments—usually extra taxes or fees—enforced by the government if you break the retirement system's rules. The two biggest ones are the **Early Withdrawal Penalty** (if you pull money out of your 401(k) or IRA before you turn 59½, the government hits you with an extra 10% tax) and the **Late Enrollment Penalty** (if you skip signing up for Medicare at age 65 when you're supposed to, your monthly insurance costs will be permanently higher for the rest of your life).

## RMD (Required Minimum Distribution)

The government gives you great tax breaks while you save for retirement, but they eventually want their tax money. An RMD is a rule that forces you to start taking a minimum amount of money out of your traditional retirement accounts every year once you reach a certain age **(70 ½, 72, 73 or 75 - depending on your birthday)**, whether you want to or not.

## Roth Account (Roth IRA / Roth 401(k)

Named after a U.S. Senator, a "Roth" account is a special tax flavor. You pay taxes on the money *before* you put it into the account. The massive benefit? The money grows, and when you take it out in retirement, you don't owe a single penny in taxes. Everything you withdraw is 100% yours.

## Roth Conversion

At its core, a **Roth conversion** is a tax strategy where you move funds from a pre-tax retirement account—like a Traditional IRA or a traditional 401(k)—into a Roth IRA.

Because you haven't paid income taxes on your traditional retirement money yet, you must report the converted amount as taxable income in the year you make the move. However, once that money lands inside the Roth IRA, it grows completely tax-free, and all future qualified withdrawals are 100% tax-free.

## Sequence of Returns Risk

Imagine you retire and immediately the stock market crashes for three years in a row. Because you have to pull money out of your accounts to buy groceries while the market is down, your savings shrink way faster than expected. This is the danger of *when* a market drop happens; a crash right at the beginning of retirement is much more dangerous than a crash 15 years later.

## Traditional Account (Traditional IRA / 401(k))

The opposite of a Roth account. You get a tax break *now*—the money you put in lowers your taxes today. However, your savings grow "tax-deferred." This means you will owe regular income taxes on every dollar you pull out of the account when you are retired.

## Vesting

If your boss promises to give you extra money toward your retirement account (a match), they usually want to make sure you don't quit the next day. "Vesting" is a timeline or probation period. For example, a company might say you are "fully vested" after 3 years. If you leave before then, the company takes back some or all of the extra money they gave you.

# All Sources

## Sources: Regrets


- https://aura.life/articles/top-regrets-of-the-dying
- https://www.theguardian.com/lifeandstyle/2012/feb/01/top-five-regrets-of-the-dying
- https://en.wikipedia.org/wiki/The_Top_Five_Regrets_of_the_Dying
- https://pmc.ncbi.nlm.nih.gov/articles/PMC8471755/
- https://pubmed.ncbi.nlm.nih.gov/19711617/
- https://www.businessinsider.com/retirement-regrets-saving-investing-loneliness-parenting-older-americans-survey-2024-12
- https://www.businessinsider.com/retirement-regrets-saving-401k-prenup-life-insurance-investing-strategies-2024-12
- https://www.ctinsider.com/living/article/older-americans-regret-health-savings-survey-22084210.php
- https://www.msn.com
- https://www.newsweek.com
- https://www.aol.com
- https://www.businessinsider.com
- https://www.moneywise.com
- https://www.ctinsider.com
- https://www.today.com/health/biggest-regrets-older-people-share-what-they-d-do-differently-t118918
- https://www.aarp.org/money/retirement/purchases-retirees-often-regret/
- https://www.aesinternational.com/blog/5-big-retirement-regrets-and-what-you-can-do-now-to-avoid-them
- https://www.youtube.com/watch?v=GpHGoYi2UHU&vl=en-US
- https://www.whitecoatinvestor.com/biggest-regrets-elderly/
- https://keenwealthadvisors.com/insights/regrets-in-retirement
- https://www.reddit.com/r/RetirementReady/comments/1o2rc00/retirement_regrets_top_15_things_retirees_wish/

- https://www.facebook.com/whichuk/posts/the-4-most-common-regrets-when-retiring-and-how-to-avoid-them/1359471332881075/
- https://www.youtube.com/watch?v=gsbbLfBB3eI
- https://www.torowealth.com.au/retirement-regrets/
- https://news.nationwide.com/recent-retirees-battle-with-unexpected-financial-challenges-regret-retirement-savings-strategies/
- https://carlsonfinancial.com/common-regrets-among-retirees-and-what-you-can-learn-from-them/
- https://www.aeaweb.org/conference/2024/program/paper/9EDD8YaT
- https://www.transamericainstitute.org/research/retirement
- https://www.businessinsider.com/4-biggest-retiree-regrets-from-financial-advisor-2025-6
- https://repository.upenn.edu/entities/publication/1d50b357-7a0d-4b5d-82d0-eb11e14e22d8
- https://www.transamericainstitute.org
- https://kerryhannon.com/?p=10221
- https://www.nber.org/papers/w30696
- https://www.transamericainstitute.org/research/retirement
- https://www.businessinsider.com/4-biggest-retiree-regrets-from-financial-advisor-2025-6
- https://repository.upenn.edu/entities/publication/1d50b357-7a0d-4b5d-82d0-eb11e14e22d8
- ... https://www.mcknightsseniorliving.com/news/retirement-income-unexpected-financial-shocks-top-list-of-concerns-among-retirees/
- https://www.transamericainstitute.org
- https://kerryhannon.com/?p=10221
- https://www.nber.org/papers/w30696
- https://www.cbsnews.com/news/retirement-inflation-health-care-costs/
- https://www.investmentnews.com/retirement-planning/retirement-uncertainty-cuts-across-generations-transamerica/261010
- https://carlsonfinancial.com/common-regrets-among-retirees-and-what-you-can-learn-from-them/
- https://www.today.com/health/biggest-regrets-older-people-share-what-they-d-do-differently-t118918
- https://www.aarp.org/money/retirement/purchases-retirees-often-regret/
- https://www.aesinternational.com/blog/5-big-retirement-regrets-and-what-you-can-do-now-to-avoid-them

- https://www.youtube.com/watch?v=GpHGoYi2UHU&vl=en-US
- https://www.whitecoatinvestor.com/biggest-regrets-elderly/
- https://keenwealthadvisors.com/insights/regrets-in-retirement
- https://www.reddit.com/r/RetirementReady/comments/1o2rc00/retirement_regrets_top_15_things_retirees_wish/
- https://www.facebook.com/whichuk/posts/the-4-most-common-regrets-when-retiring-and-how-to-avoid-them/1359471332881075/
- https://www.youtube.com/watch?v=gsbbLfBB3eI
- https://www.torowealth.com.au/retirement-regrets/
- https://news.nationwide.com/recent-retirees-battle-with-unexpected-financial-challenges-regret-retirement-savings-strategies/
- https://www.aeaweb.org/conference/2024/program/paper/9EDD8YaT


# Sources: Golden Rules


- https://www.ebri.org/retirement/retirement-confidence-survey
- https://www.transamericainstitute.org/research/publications/details/retirees-enjoying-life-amid-health-and-financial-uncertainties
- https://crr.bc.edu/a-review-of-existing-measures-of-retirement-well-being/
- https://www.fidelity.com/learning-center/wealth-management-insights/sources-of-happiness-in-retirement
- https://www.transamericainstitute.org
- https://www.transamericainstitute.org/research/retirement-realities-the-experience-of-retirees
- https://greenwaldresearch.com
- https://www.ebri.org
- https://www.lifehealth.com
- https://finance.yahoo.com
- https://www.fidelity.com/viewpoints/retirement/retirement-satisfaction
- https://www.fidelity.com/viewpoints/retirement/retiree-health-care-costs
- https://www.transamericacenter.org
- https://www.aarp.org/retirement
- https://www.ncbi.nlm.nih.gov/pmc/articles/PMC6179761
- https://www.ncbi.nlm.nih.gov/pmc/articles/PMC8471755
- https://www.cnbc.com/2024/06/20/what-retirees-say-they-would-do-differently.html
- https://www.ifa.com/articles/retirees_biggest_successes_and_regrets
- https://www.morningstar.com/retirement

- https://www.milkeninstitute.org/content-hub/research-and-reports/reports
- https://www.fidelity.com/viewpoints/retirement/retirement-satisfaction
- https://www.ncbi.nlm.nih.gov/pmc/articles/PMC6179761
- https://www.ncbi.nlm.nih.gov/pmc/articles/PMC8471755
- https://www.cnbc.com/2024/06/20/what-retirees-say-they-would-do-differently.html
- https://www.aarp.org/retirement
- https://www.morningstar.com/retirement
- https://www.asppa-net.org/news/2024/11/retirees-biggest-joys-and-regrets-in-post-pandemic-times/
- https://villagewalkseniorliving.com/10-best-retirement-hobby-suggestions-and-more-for-seniors/
- https://www.nia.nih.gov/health/healthy-aging/participating-activities-you-enjoy-you-age
- https://www.amavidaliving.com/blog/exciting-things-to-do-in-retirement/
- https://www.ebri.org/retirement/retirement-confidence-survey/1996-survey-results/retirement-not-the-golden-age-for-all
- https://legacy.trincoll.edu/retirement

- https://www.asppa-nct.org/news/2024/11/retirees-biggest-joys-and-regrets-in-post-pandemic-times/
- https://villagewalkseniorliving.com/10-best-retirement-hobby-suggestions-and-more-for-seniors/
- https://legacy.trincoll.edu/retirement
- https://pmc.ncbi.nlm.nih.gov/articles/PMC10124805/
- https://www.nia.nih.gov/health/healthy-aging/participating-activities-you-enjoy-you-age
- https://www.nia.nih.gov/sites/default/files/2017-06/health_and_retirement_study_0.pdf
- https://www.youtube.com/watch?v=mNUSJ3juAbA
- https://www.amavidaliving.com/blog/exciting-things-to-do-in-retirement/
- https://www.ebri.org/retirement/retirement-confidence-survey/1996-survey-results/retirement-not-the-golden-age-for-all
- https://www.annuity.org/retirement/lifestyle/retirement-bucket-list/

# Sources: Checklist


- https://www.dol.gov/agencies/ebsa/about-ebsa/our-activities/resource-center/publications/retirement-savings-toolkit
- https://www.ameripriseadvisors.com/kelman-magliari-advisory-group/pre-retirement-planning-checklist
- https://investor.vanguard.com/investor-resources-education/retirement/planning-checklist
- https://www.ssa.gov/benefits/retirement
- https://www.medicare.gov
- https://wealthvieu.com/retirement-financial-checklist
- https://www.ssa.gov/
- https://www.ssa.gov/myaccount/
- https://www.ssa.gov/medicare/apply.html
- https://www.ssa.gov/medicare/plan/when-to-sign-up
- https://www.fidelity.com/learning-center/personal-finance/5-moves-before-retirement
- https://www.fidelity.com/viewpoints/retirement/countdown-to-retirement
- https://www.fidelity.com/retirement-planning/retirement-checklist-wrap-up
- https://www.kiplinger.com/retirement/retirement-plans/checklist-for-retirement-planning
- https://www.kiplinger.com/retirement/retirement-planning/start-refining-your-income-plan-5-years-before-retirement
- https://www.american.edu/hr/benefits/retirement/upload/a-pr-0320-checklist.pdf
- https://www.calpers.ca.gov/members/retirement-benefits/service-disability-retirement/retirement-planning-checklist

- https://www.edwardjones.com/us-en/market-news-insights/retirement/preparing/retirement-checklist
- https://empeople.com/learn/empeople-insights/retirement-checklist-the-5-years-before-you-retire/
- https://www.dol.gov/sites/dolgov/files/ebsa/about-ebsa/our-activities/resource-center/publications/retirement-toolkit.pdf
- https://www.unifiedlegacyadvisors.com/blog/the-10-5-and-1-year-retirement-planning-checklist
- https://investor.vanguard.com/investor-resources-education/retirement/planning-retirement-checklist
- https://www.neamb.com/retirement-planning/preretirement-checklist)
- https://workplace.schwab.com/learning-center/pre-retirement-playbook)
- https://reedmckinneygroup.bairdwealth.com/resource-center/retirement/the-pre-retirement-checklist)
- https://www.presbyterianliving.org/blog/pre-retirement-checklist/
- https://reedmckinneygroup.bairdwealth.com/resource-center/retirement/the-pre-retirement-checklist
- https://www.usa.gov/retirement-planning-tools
- https://smartasset.com/retirement/retirement-prep-checklist
- https://www.drs.wa.gov/life/retire/check/
- https://www.kiplinger.com/retirement/retirement-plans/checklist-for-retirement-planning
- https://www.brighthousefinancial.com/education/retirement-planning/ready-to-retire-retirement-checklist/
- https://www.ssa.gov/benefits/medicare/medicare-premiums.html

- https://www.ssa.gov/pubs/EN-05-10035.pdf
- https://www.ssa.gov/medicare
- thttps://www.usbank.com/retirement-planning/financial-perspectives/retirement-planning-checklist.html
- https://www.ameriprise.com/financial-goals-priorities/retirement/retirement-countdown
- https://www.guardianlife.com/retirement-checklist
- https://www.boldin.com/retirement/yearly-retirement-checklist/
- https://www.aarp.org/money/retirement/year-end-financial-checklist/
- https://moderawealth.com/planning-for-retirement/
- https://www.principal.com/individuals/learn/helpful-retirement-planning-checklist


## Sources and Citations - Retirement Vision


- https://www.fidelity.com/
- https://www.vanderbilt.edu/
- https://www.athene.com/smart-strategies


## Sources & Citations for Age 55 - Milestones


- https://www.irs.gov/retirement-plans/hardships-early-withdrawals-and-loans
- https://www.fidelity.com/learning-center/personal-finance/what-is-rule-of-55
- https://www.fidelity.com/learning-center/personal-finance/72t-rule
- https://smartasset.com/retirement/how-to-avoid-tax-on-457-withdrawal

# Sources & Citations - Social Security Ages - Milestones

- https://www.ssa.gov/benefits/retirement/planner/1960.html
- https://www.ssa.gov/benefits/retirement/planner/agereduction.html
- https://www.ssa.gov/benefits/retirement/planner/delayret.html

# Sources & Citations Medicare - Milestones

- https://www.ssa.gov/benefits/medicare/medicare-premiums.html
- https://www.medicare.gov/basics/costs/medicare-costs
- https://www.aarp.org/social-security/faq/income-affect-medicare-premium/
- https://www.ssa.gov/medicare/plan/when-to-sign-up
- https://www.medicare.gov/basics/costs/medicare-costs/avoid-penalties
- https://www.medicareinteractive.org/understanding-medicare/medicare-prescription-drug-coverage-part-d/medicare-part-d-enrollment/part-d-late-enrollment-penalties
- https://www.medicareresources.org/medicare-eligibility-and-enrollment/important-dates/

# Sources & Citations - QCD - Milestones

- https://www.schwab.com/learn/story/reducing-rmds-with-qcds
- https://www.fidelitycharitable.org/guidance/philanthropy/qualified-charitable-distribution.html

- https://www.northerntrust.com/united-states/institute/articles/qualified-charitable-distributions
- https://www.irs.gov/publications/p526


# Sources & Citations RMD - Milestones


- https://www.irs.gov/retirement-plans/retirement-plan-and-ira-required-minimum-distributions-faqs
- https://www.irs.gov/publications/p590b
- https://www.fidelity.com/building-savings/learn-about-iras/rmd
- https://www.thrivent.com/insights/retirement-planning/rmds-by-age-understanding-how-distributions-change-as-you-get-older


# Sources and Citations – Biggest Regret


- https://www.federalreserve.gov/econres/scfindex.htm
- https://www.fidelity.com/learning-center/personal-finance/average-retirement-savings
(Fidelity Investments)
- https://iadviser.com/average-retirement-savings-by-age-2026/
- https://www.journeyadvisory.group/blog/retirement-savings-by-age-2026
(Journey Advisory Group, LLC)
- https://www.investopedia.com/how-much-americans-ages-65-to-74-have-saved-for-retirement-and-what-it-means-11993419
- https://www.investopedia.com/retirement-savings-for-55-64-year-olds-navigating-surprising-financial-challenges-during-the-final-working-years-11993429
- https://web.stanford.edu/~wfsharpe/retecon/4percent.pdf

- https://en.wikipedia.org/wiki/Trinity_study
- https://retirementresearcher.com/safe-withdrawal-rates-for-retirement-and-the-trinity-study/
- https://www.kitces.com/blog/guyton-klinger-guardrails-retirement-income-rules-risk-based/
- https://www.pyrfordfp.com/post/using-the-guyton-klinger-withdrawal-guardrails-for-retirement-income
- https://www.morningstar.com/retirement/morningstars-retirement-income-research-finding-your-safe-withdrawal-rate
- https://thepoorswiss.com/updated-trinity-study/
- https://www.kitces.com/blog/guyton-klinger-guardrails-retirement-income-rules-risk-based/
- https://goodlifewealth.com/guardrails-withdrawal-strategy-2/
- https://www.paestateplanners.com/blog/die-with-zero-by-bill-perkins-a-different-view-on-gifting-spending-retirement-and-estate-plannin.cfm (
- https://www.kiplinger.com/retirement/retirement-planning/the-die-with-zero-rule-of-retirement
- https://hurlowwealth.com/blogs/lessons-from-die-with-zero-getting-all-you-can-from-your-money-and-your-life-by-bill-perkins/
- https://www.whitecoatinvestor.com/die-with-zero-criticism/
- https://www.kitces.com/blog/category/12-weekend-reading/
- https://www.morningstar.com/podcasts/the-long-view/66cd6d3f-109d-4db5-b464-0de11bdf3364
- https://www.vanguardinvestor.co.uk/articles/latest-thoughts/retirement/how-to-make-your-pension-last-and-your-retirement-enjoyable
- https://retirementresearcher.com/what-is-a-safety-first-retirement-plan/

- https://www.kitces.com/blog/modified-required-minimum-distributions-rmd-swr-safe-withdrawal-rate-method-portfolio-retirement-income-paycheck-irs/
- https://www.advisorperspectives.com/articles/2022/03/03/the-intuition-for-reverse-mortgages
- **https://www.fidelity.com/viewpoints/retirement/how-much-do-i-need-to-retire**
- **https://www.fidelity.com/learning-center/personal-finance/when-can-i-retire**
- **https://www.fidelity.com/viewpoints/retirement/retirement-income-sources**
- **https://www.troweprice.com/personal-investing/resources/insights/retirement-savings-by-age-what-to-do-with-your-portfolio.html**
- **https://smartasset.com/retirement/25x-retirement-rule**
- **https://www.bankrate.com/retirement/retirement-rules-to-know/**
- **https://www.thepeoples.com/how-much-do-i-need-to-save-for-retirement](https://www.thepeoples.com/how-much-do-i-need-to-save-for-retirement)**
- **https://www.fidelity.com/viewpoints/retirement/how-much-money-should-I-save](https://www.fidelity.com/viewpoints/retirement/how-much-money-should-I-save)**
- **https://www.troweprice.com/personal-investing/resources/insights/youre-age-35-50-or-60-how-much-saved-for-retirement.html](https://www.troweprice.com/personal-investing/resources/insights/youre-age-35-50-or-60-how-much-saved-for-retirement.html)**
- **https://www.nerdwallet.com/investing/calculators/retirement-calculator](https://www.nerdwallet.com/investing/calculators/retirement-calculator)**

- https://investor.vanguard.com/tools-calculators/retirement-income-calculator](https://investor.vanguard.com/tools-calculators/retirement-income-calculator)

- https://www.bankrate.com/retirement/retirement-plan-calculator/](https://www.bankrate.com/retirement/retirement-plan-calculator/)

- https://www.nerdwallet.com/investing/calculators/retirement-calculator

- https://www.bankrate.com/retirement/retirement-plan-calculator/

- https://www.umcu.org/learn/resources/calculators/how-long-will-my-retirement-savings-last-calculator

- https://www.thepeoples.com/how-much-do-i-need-to-save-for-retirement

- https://investor.vanguard.com/tools-calculators/retirement-income-calculator
- https://www.fidelity.com/viewpoints/retirement/how-much-money-should-I-save

- https://www.merrilledge.com/retirement/personal-retirement-calculator

- https://www.troweprice.com/personal-investing/resources/insights/youre-age-35-50-or-60-how-much-saved-for-retirement.html

- https://www.tiaa.org/public/tools-calculators
- https://retirenumber.com/calculators/4-percent-rule

- https://www.smartasset.com/retirement/retirement-calculator

- https://www.northwesternmutual.com/life-and-money/retirement-savings-rules-of-thumb/

- https://www.wsj.com/buyside/personal-finance/financial-advisors/whats-your-retirement-number
- https://www.freefincalc.net/retirement-calculator
- https://retirenumber.com
- https://www.the-sun.com/money/16036649/new-bucket-strategy-make-savings-last-retirement/
- https://www.kiplinger.com/retirement/retirement-planning/the-4-rule-gets-a-closer-look

# Sources – Terms and Acronyms

- https://www.irs.gov/retirement-plans
- https://www.ssa.gov/
- https://www.cms.gov/
- https://www.investor.gov/
- https://www.aicpa-cima.com/
- https://www.letsmakeaplan.org/
- https://www.irs.gov/e-file-providers/definition-of-adjusted-gross-income
- https://www.irs.gov/credits-deductions/modified-adjusted-gross-income
- https://www.ssa.gov/benefits/retirement/planner/ageincrease.html
- https://www.dol.gov/agencies/ebsa/workers-and-families/changing-jobs-and-retirement

# Sources ISP


- https://www.bogleheads.org/wiki/Investment_policy_statement
- https://corporate.vanguard.com/content/dam/corp/research/pdf/vanguards_principles_for_investing_success.pdf
- https://www.definefinancial.com/wp-content/uploads/2020/02/Sample-Institutional-IPS.pdf
- https://www.financialfinesse.com/2018/06/28/how-to-create-your-own-investment-policy-statement-and-why-its-important/
- https://www.centralbank.net/learning-center/survey-finds-americans-need-more-retirement-planning-knowledge/


# Sources Unintended Consequences


- https://www.cms.gov/newsroom/fact-sheets/2026-medicare-parts-b-premiums-deductibles
- https://www.ssa.gov/benefits/medicare/medicare-premiums.html
- https://www.kiplinger.com/retirement/medicare/medicare-premiums-2026-irmaa-brackets-and-surcharges-for-parts-b-and-d
- https://aspe.hhs.gov/sites/default/files/documents/dd73d4f00d8a819d10b2fdb70d254f7b/detailed-guidelines-2025.pdf
- https://www.federalregister.gov/documents/2025/01/17/2025-01377/annual-update-of-the-hhs-poverty-guidelines
- https://www.kff.org/interactive/subsidy-calculator/
- https://www.boldin.com/retirement/retiring-at-62-early-retirement-health-costs/

## Sources Power of Compounding

- https://fi.edu/en/support/benjamin-franklins-donor-story
- https://surface.syr.edu/hst_etd/30/
- https://www.elderlawanswers.com/benjamin-franklins-estate-planning-lessons-21442
- https://www.wife.org/a-penny-saved.htm

# Sources – Power of Inflation

- https://www.officialdata.org/1990-dollars-in-2025
- https://www.officialdata.org/us/inflation/1990
- https://www.officialdata.org/us/inflation/1990?amount=1990&endYear=2025
- https://www.in2013dollars.com/Eggs/price-inflation/1990-to-2025
- https://www.dollartimes.com/inflation/items/price-of-a-gallon-of-gas-in-1990
- https://www.in2013dollars.com/gasoline-%28all-types%29/price-inflation/1990-to-2025
- https://www.natoonline.org/data/ticket-price
- https://www.wdwmagic.com
- https://disneyworld.disney.go.com
- https://www.starbucks.com
- https://corporate.mcdonalds.com
- https://www.economist.com/big-mac-index
- https://www.costco.com
- https://www.toyota.com

- https://www.edmunds.com
- https://www.ford.com
- https://www.edmunds.com
- https://www.uga.edu
- https://oir.uga.edu
- https://fred.stlouisfed.org
- https://www.census.gov

# Final Thoughts

First, thank you so much for taking the time to read this book. It is my prayer that this has been a blessing to you and your family.

Secondly, if you have an opportunity to send me an e-mail with your thoughts, comments or suggestions, that would be very helpful.

Finally, I hope you were encouraged and strengthened by what you read.

**paulbeersdorf@gmail.com**

Blessings to you and your family!

**Paul Beersdorf**

www.ingramcontent.com/pod-product-compliance
Lightning Source LLC
Chambersburg PA
CBHW050526240926
51846CB00003B/709
* 9 7 8 1 9 7 1 3 4 4 0 5 8 *